OCCASIONAL PIECES

Feynman Poly

OCCASIONAL PIECES

Feynman Poly

FLOREAT SYSTEMS
PUBLICATIONS
BENIN CITY

Printed by:
Floreat Systems
Catholic Archdiocese of Benin Printing Press
30, Airport Road,
Benin City, Edo State, Nigeria
08133967455

Appreciation

Thanks to God Almighty,
And also, thanks to Mr. and Mrs. Isaac and
Clementina IGBUKU for inspiring me
throughout my writing.
And also, thanks to
Very Rev. Father Ben Brodricks
for his massive support.

<u>FOREWORD</u>

A gliding wonder which takes us to the shore of the deepest feelings. Aren't you enthralled to discover the fumes of diverse emotions?

Here comes the poetic wonder in many genres named "OCCASIONAL PIECES" from an eminent poet Feynman Poly from Nigeria. Every page you turn, it resonates with a bundle of feelings so pure and blissful. Your soul will wander in the forests of questions once unsolved creating a mysterious journey through his book. As a writer, the poet is efficient and well versed. The dictions within his collection of poems speak about his versatility. Every poems are a baggage of soulful mantras and experiences which each one of us could have experienced once in our lives.

Granules of love ceramics once broke is mended to form an epitome of unearthed feelings. Beguiling thoughts and riveting poetry enchants our minds.

Happy Reading

Vandana Sudheesh
Author of "THE HUMBLE WRATH"

Contents

<u>THE HOUR IS NOT A SLOT</u>

The radio had to build her as the television had the capacity and the
broadcasting in such inserted prime hours to the listeners of
profanity that delays no bloopers of censors but nudity had to live
in the other places of dedicated and you desirable but later had the
material that worked with the time zone of plus and time sniffing
had to record him like a video whose device's inbox him the tape
that she never understand but recorders had the zeros like
cables seeing the segments of the television come to pause, but
as the music continues to be detected I see.
Talent competitions becoming unaware of the zones in the
world of a normal to random but modules in acres must put me
in the memory of the last, I do jump.
Kilobits had become the latter and bleep noise as listeners to
me or other known presence had substitute sound for an
addition or convenience.

Copyright by Feynman poly

Should I call you in the presence of love I see you as the prophets
that keeps me bare but my feet had no shame .
Ok let my feeds I had no fear so I likely heads to my hearth,
it seems cutting roadways is not easy but see trains focus on me.

Copyright by Feynman poly

THE IMPLICATIONS HAD CARRIED.....

In dialogue of Socratic man,
As compositions or dates whose early has whatsoever pan.
Has authors with stages knows the early can.
She uses me as a development of philosophical swan.
She sees classifications but thematic had terms barn.
As my Plato must conclude a reason to know Han,
she directs the sets of Parmenides but Socrates Hassan
kisses to Socrates go apart, but I stand the Wlan.

Copyright by Feynman poly.

LISTEN TO THE SPIRIT THAT CARRIED YOUR BRAIN.

He catches the fortified towers that dictate the dawn of yawn,
and voices of the surrendered minds that resolved psyched time,
as Sabbaths brains with end turns the indignations attentions
whose rejected flap lime.
Downs or ups, of world sea anchors the exalted fly with violently
intentions crime .
The festivaled pockets had turn eggs as priests life's whose
virgins hits slime.

Copyright by Feynman poly.

STAY AWAY FOR YOU WILL NOT FIND KNOWLEDGEABLE FOOLS.

The absence of you had granted me no grants but you have
disappointed the Eddy at the gates.
She discovers a new place in me to extract and keep me.
She stays by starving to pay attentions as the preterition had me
dim my laughs .
My insanity had to disappear and she goes out quietly but I went
off with evidence makes no man stupid ,the night
had to pass ,I went down like the agoraphobia that becomes shy
to wake.
Her nature had to be calm but I have to lay you by force.
Copyright by Feynman poly.

SHE IS PAYING THE HEAD MATRIX GUILT...

As mathematics of a man had to obey rectangular array but I
have to say
that the columns had raised me an acceptable symbols that
moreover had the expressions to be shaken .
The rows had afflicted me with the columns of calamity to watch
the subscripts of you taken but added an act of salutations
whose confirmations rides me in with an open scaler that
inspires me the commutatives of people but I had to cease
rotations with lies and the squares had to bear me witness.
Copyright by Feynman poly.

<u>Blood from the Tourney Queen</u>

Courson had to see his cousin of Duke and the floods of times has
lost me in menorrhea of no menstrual blood whose Mathras
and Chamberlain had greengage the knight of my pardon at
paspy of times .
As Devon of the Juno had the free Adventists of his Apollyon but
the good aureole of the Camelot had me but Carlos sees no cats to
the coinage of the rings of corvee.

Copyright by Feynman poly.

<u>Fiction</u>

Vectors had the electrons at space but my derivations of linear
space were like reactivity of numbers that had the atoms of
rational numbers that provided the planar that had fields of
rings and the definitions of concepts and axioms shares good
structures of topology like a reagent as a continuity of atom but
distance had to observe that orders and products are usually
equatorially a mixtures of skew portions .

Reference read: vector algebra

Copyright by Feynman poly.

*A refined gold of peace which had become precious to me like
beautiful stones had ends to pursue.*

<u>FICTION</u>

All men had a kind of peace like a watchman that won the
Pulitzer Prize in the sea of thoughts.
Dissolutions are detestable but of much crimes of the realistic
remnants in the Ottoman empire had forefathers and during
which, the queens of heavens the world war one pour the cedars.
And I embellished the burned of the natures of the drastic places
of past that changes like speaking in that oracle of life and
widely believing her peace had praised you of nothing but if
Richard Holbrooke had to come as he took you on a book of a
place that dies out in the shelters of our ruins.

The swords of the middle cakes made your ways towards east
of the wastelands but all as offer you a silver of anger ,the result
had to bring you closer to enlightened presence of senses.
But my pains had to be challenged by the juices of the times that
fell into the river.

Copyright by Feynman poly.

<u>Because of the Indian reservations just as shoulders.</u>

Because of the Indian reservations just as shoulders lands
managed the place of a cut as native America tribes had
stretched like federally recognized tribes whose wilderness lands
allotments had been detested like tri balance hearths in the
graves.
But individuals went down to the pits of enclaves so powerful
like Rhodes islands whose shoulders hibernates treaty of love
and speaks tribal sovereignty to remove them to the loads of
casinos in the thwarts.
As tourists of stars both the duress had joined me in the Phoenix
of bullocks but Los Angeles had to pronounce the Southern New
Jersey, as a name of memorial.

Poetry and prose.
Copyright by Feynman Poly

HOPE
FICTION

After my linear algebra I decided to see mathematics as the sons whose linear equations went down but Euclidean plane had its tongues and linear maps whose body and vector spaces had man and matrix had to ablaze if geometry knows tomorrow.
But lines of hers brags and the planes had today rotations that went away and rises the functional analysis of kings and kingdoms .
Her engineering had to approve the modelling of a clean slit but non-linear systems had to work to fulfil differentials that tried the multivariates of murders and functions with bids that splendid.
My coordinates had crowns and determinants becomes a man of Grammar's rules that recites Scriptures and complex planes may speak faults .

Copyright by Feynman poly.

OSTEOLYSIS AS MAN...

Prose poetry.

And of those cities of whose deaths had the priests always by the kings that sweareth ye like bacterials at tumults whose of the heart had the tissues to rejoice .
Of what use is the tooth loss whose little joys had abscess that sings the strings.
Like sjogren makes his lips a place of syndromes that makes one upon a great cementum that thou provided a simple place to common sugar until I pray for your saliva to light you up not as diabetes headest thou the antihistamines of that mighty ways whose toothpastes beeds thou welcome.

Copyright by Feynman poly.

AS PROLACTIN IS BECOMING...

The inhabited modulators of what she sweeps as secretions had to pursue me to the pituitary servants that I enrolled .
Your hormones is righteous, Oh Bintu whose prolactin had afflicted himself of the anterior presence of imaginations .

If bromocriptine had Hooves as hyperprolactinemia had to sing to her agonists that persuade me to save Cabergoline as a comforter.
As analogous pains whose inhibitors were like sure infertility of horns and as dysfunctions may have it ,no failures had me to prick of lactations of love at hand.

Copyright by Feynman poly.

<u>EXAMINATIONS AND ITS HUMBLE SPIRITS...</u>

Prose Poetry

Of evaluations must declare the dental evidence to the sinners of criminal justice whose house of human remains had no peace as race has healed by the occupations of not angers but socio-economic status in the shoulders of the teeth our hearth and people.

Is radiographs a built up of photographs among the Torah of DNA whose stretches had crime scenes of the backs of stabs national academy of science will retain as the legal proceedings to rejoice in sexual assault but by trees had murder of insolence and the tissues of the pills of stones stomach and the spoils of the buttocks had raised the devils to strike.

Copyright by Feynman poly.

I AM SATURATED...

With diagrams so good to draw him,
As her atoms of carbons had seven even holy hydrocarbons sim.
My structures are cyclic her branches as linear firm.
My frameworks had basics and molecules to draw the kim.
Her acids is reactive, polished carboxylic my right hand
Ketones both having answered slim.
If molecules is same your groups will become the wages of
functional hymn.
I got a problem but purpose rhythm.
But realistically as structures of simple splendours of drawings
zim.
Your names had rules if I go away just stearwarm swim.
You suggested the molecules by representing zeal ,
But time linearly like solutions had branched my unrealistic
hydrocarbons bill.

My options are cyclic,
My thoughts are possibilities of chapter shad deal.

Copyright at Feynman poly
Chemistry humanities

<u>My eyes have gaze...</u>

You lonely like tyrants that plays my will to dwell.
But fairly and unfair you are same.
If you lead my time by resting,
As remembrance excels.
My winter is strength hideous at summer.
Prayers confounds those leaves were dusty like frosts that checks the saps of life.
My snowed is beauty but gone so quite long.
An anointed bareness as prisoners of liquids left me no distillations and summers faces .
Some effects is beauty like glasses and walls that bereft my flowers is resemblance.

She meets my winter so distilled but still her substances had show I lease when glory is sweet and my life as a king.

Copyright by Feynman poly.

<u>As heaven is such a boring place...</u>

As some people with tribal marks are going to hell soon.
But to bad we are not going to heaven with the pun.
so I say thank God for that who would want to go to heaven with
the fun zoon.
Oh room,
I will accept island inshallah you will go in heaven boom.
And hell fire,
and how many feet less people are shorter lire,
I see you all in hell I guess sire but why cry?
Seriously I will change my ways of life fly.

Copyright by Feynman poly

<u>Age is thine....</u>

But windows wrinkles and despites to see,
I remembered you alive as time is golden.
What dies is images, I am single to die.
You spent loveliness,
But unthriftly my legacy is beauty, myself had lived upon.
who is nothing should me as bequests natures.
Who lent Frank a being,
Had lent no niggard as beauteous,
Freely I largess no abuses as usurers,
Must give a use,
Love is not profitless I give but yet much sums,
You are great but alone no self but traffics you have.

Copyright by Feynman poly

<u>SHE SHINES LIKE SUCCESSION........</u>

As arts has made me new,
I feel so warm with blood and I see you beguile the renewest but prosperity had stop my tombs of wills and folds
With prosperity had stopped,
Like prime and April is lovely to come back with a call.
My wombs is unheard and fair oh husbandry,
And tillage had disdains.

Copyright by Feynman poly.

<u>ROCK AND ROLL.........</u>

She loves me she loves my enemies,
I look at the city,
The city of love is filled with treasures,
She gives me offerings and spoke to me.
Not to abandon the hearth and its laws,
She is life and a horror so I was careful to make use of her treasures I reside in her body ,
A sound so real amplified me like reciting Shakespeare's sonnets in rock and roll.

Copyright by Feynman poly.

<u>HOW MY FRIENDS AND MY WIND WENT DOWN.......</u>

To see death even before you cry like a friend to see how times lived In the sky ,even before you see me pretend to say yes,
then you must be free like cannon balls that answer my ears even before she washed many heads ,
The man exist like the wind that knows me in the sleeps that works to say yes to the white roads and the mountains like flying sands lived before I banned you and like answers that exist when crowds pretend before his years came to say yes to me then I had to turn the winds it takes and some people sees ,the blowing in some winds that calls the answers that says,
Yes to the banned forever, but looks I walk with roads before man had called you ,and banned life forever to have her winds before my seas had washed me to say yes to the free and till I see death that cries as people and the friends sees free people with wind that allow me the doves of sleeps.

Copyright by Feynman poly.

<u>SUFFERINGS TO PRAISE.</u>

Aside of raining presence so sharp but he lives,
On me with understandings that reads with moments of dismiss
always along the nights of a roar splits of rocks so needed by thy
grace not against the disciple boys of memories to depart no
roles from seashells had the lips that adlip me of foam that
becomes rich to give a gift that rises a place of knowledge with
experienced groin of sufferings whose written phosphorescent
Phoenix had shoots that is looking for me to praise him in the
cascades of not just the dishonest of stars but to save him to
nestle along the presence of their hopes that begs for mercy until
the madness of life and ivory moments had ends when the
crooks of the white temples preserves a god that should dissolve
the drunken In the inhabitants of coastlands.
If rain and the offices that in all from the clothe of flesh will went,
about with he that grows chrysanthemum revellers with the
roots of heavy fishes.

Copyright by Feynman poly.

MY SMILES ARE MY CRIES

My smiles are my cries often like the smoke of love and its graves had the breasts as the lands of which are for me to bear.
But like when she crushed me inside with a great resort then she is dear to me by making me as a city whose kingdoms of cedars can never get me confuse to express my desires of emotions that is of no fight but love is a secret noise at the gates of smiles that never laments but had the master a time that bore my organs like a good man with the built headphones of love and ivory listens to me again but of great values like Solomon is beautiful.
To listen to the head of love for so long in itself but love and its calamity had shoulders that we must climb but of a gain that see the yokes of its forth sense.

Copyright by Feynman poly

History.

Prose Poetry

Psychology had to report you to the presence of research whose home can be impractical but the psychologist whose challenges had accept these schools of Harvard's like laws that hard to become the functional wills of good ideas.

My schools had her proceedings but nonetheless the causes is truly an official post to be until settings were withnesses to many years of illness.

A century of expert has directors that has upheld the imbue whose time must see approach comes like decisions as condescending is not only enough for health and the board sees her illness in the community of scrutinizations that in time like Americans becoming yellowish to be untouched or even exaggerated to backlas.

Copyright by Feynman poly

Look in the presence of my justice for thy glasses had to control the lightening and tell me not to be the companion which the face had been like days thou viewest my looks to the swords that now is the tone to creed the tune for her benefits sees how fine that face looks like .
I should form the morals of mortals whom another whose presence finds wanting like fresh repairs that tells the story of her speech is now climbing the candles ,but thou not even the horses had my renewest gates like beards whose thou dost sees as harmful .
She beguiled the bristled of my recognitions when words umbles had no fear of some mother's that fall upon me,
as for where I live,
Let me whisper who is she that loves them so fair from the envy sides whose unheard broke my apart in the wombs disdains to cause me pains.

Copyright at Feynman poly

Because they knew I had what will add us something for many
days I keep you inside me,
And years gone by as she is of life that had commandments in her
place of power ,
Whose eyes of time even atheist God and crowns, sees man in
doubt.

Forensic poetry .
Fortified files.
Prose and poetry
Copyright at Webster's fox.

Documentary of my life had to be a forensic kind of tower in the
science of an enemy and the violent life had been drawn but
crimes were like square of whose firm rise sleep deep on my
sides*.
If Peter Thomas has the second past whose documentary of clean
carpets had to be true all the time but ad vineyards of crimes
had the deals to rides*.
my lists were like locusts that were of much chiefs and the
episodes were rather alive to cross the deep like disobedient
sheep's and fire that sure I confides*.
You cannot live Babylon for me with a train in heaven to always
wreck my springs up the extreme doubts of no evidence as the
sun shines in the voices of darkness to always see covers and
task makers that hides*.
My networks settled on earth but the takers are empty like the
FBI agents had to shut his files like a fool in the cold of no signs at
ease of my case had to obey laws like the firm in the gates of noir

that brings you to the scene of life and investigations had to be a rapport of sides*.

Gospel of persistent output as credo has carried no infusion of dogmas whose daily belief was watered.

Copyright by Feynman poly

Concepts of notions.

Fevers like influential ideas ,
Sulphonamides or concepts,
dose tablets as conceptualization's,
Hosts transmissions since believes.
Severe and slower to consideration's,
Relapses which has hypothesis,
Can be used for perceptions.
Severe hepatics or sentiments trimesters malarias in minds eyes,
Balance leading to philosophy,
chronic used to reduce cogitations.
Cause heparin and angles,
Lists vasopressors such pictures.
Copyright by Feynman poly

<u>UNDERWORLD TWINS</u>

Literature

Devils of the ultimate mobs of my place had the twins that loads my shades of skies across the Tantalus that tried to see Zeus In the survival of bikers reds and blues.
Of bind winds of war and the baunamonites had bees of the Edoms of swarms and whose Ethan had almost the melanoscopes of Benfey as dreams and rockers were dead in the hereditary of fames of Alabama to dream about Castor and pollux had to give folktales of Lynch and even along the lablab of beeches of whose Martin's sees its adaptations in knackered.
But like the jaundice of her intuitive had hammered me no boards or gripe in the house of glass like snakes of hammered winters in the grip ancients of Lazarus .
Curtain.

Copyright by Feynman poly

BOILING POT.

Prose Poetry

A boiling hot kind of returns whose boiling pots must not abandon the broiling hot eyes of nomad as adjoining lots in the lands sets an adjoining plot of evil to a city of boiling tar not afraid of what to say in the boiling point of daughters in the hearts of melting pots like Zion in the cooking pots of prostitutes.

The smoking pots of priests and to love the boiling heats that helps me struck the adjoining parts of a woman that keeps toiling at month with a steaming pot of words that had sailing of calamities and many yacht of sheep's had attentions selling hot juices of a circle by taking pot of worm holes in the boiling fats that went back the broiling heat like perfections .
But recoiling at who forgets me as kill shots of dreams with boiling meats had spoken the deep adjoining plots that steals the baking pot of love In Euphrates of ceiling shot kissing behind a foreign prevailing spot without you satisfying the seething pot with a two face selling pots of loud flocks spilling hot presence of quarrelsome hanging pot of lutes in a place toiling hard to keep me of being caught of a lion but getting caught like crowns of oils imports the taunts of Ellicott to lead me to having caught my worth in the Callicott of curse whose prayers of Mallinckrodt had a king by selling cost the killed of rah.
If noise inputs a stone like the tooling cost went down but folding cot a guilty man.
my drilling cost your majesty a rolling cart to dash me the oil inlets of a place in the mailing cost of life but what an appalling cost to trap another hardship of boiling salt that sees me In the

boiling pitch of sounds and knifes of employing none of the souths
fiery but broiling pan was wayward like iron boiling stock my
distress whose adjoining bar will return to me like a boiling pan
to watch me at the doors of choisis par of chariots.
Copyright by Feynman poly

FORLORN BUT STUMBLES…

Together had gone beyond the apples of dawn to live the
holds of one reality whose idols must scorn like Israel had the
baton of who declares the hurting of an icon that had kept you
to take on the readings of life .
Canton had been corrupt but he hang on in delays by trusting the
yawn of an enemy that had worn so long a blind to live upon the
cry of war.
Pylons of islands that had to call on the seas of the doubts and
chiffon whose creatures has assemble to dwell on who reads me
afar from logon like rain of results and Croydon must keep me to
eggs on our line that reads monogon like an art on paper.

Copyright by Feynman poly

MY RECEPTORS ARE SLEEPING.

Prose Poetry

Nose of my examinations is sweet in between opponents of touch and justice of your dad whose fine linens had ears of response and requests.
Link the Charlots of a railway and a fruitage had telephones of fortresses and disputes of smells in the cage to decide the odours of same light.
Cradle my hates of real awards and enemies of a client must favour no broadcast that turns exhaust to lift no delays as fellows brinks a regulation from a man that declared a hat rounded up.

Curtain.
Copyright by Feynman poly

LASTLY ONCE WHEN HE SPOKE DUGS.

Prose Poetry

Uzziah with a slave of turn and murderers of his roads has baskets of a cross with loaves of her sayings Icarus must had learn to exist beyond strongholds that occurs in the drakes. Levels lived in the place of a downright made of food and has done much evils to a specific points that could be a whirling who must see peace and support the glooms of falsehood and see the distress to make the prostitutes a past of which countersigns like bears of highly esteemed ruin lived my vengeance as a game of loins and benefits of money blows like inheritance to find a holy man at the pile of dim light.

Copyright by Feynman poly

GLUTTONS AS HARMS.

Prose Poetry

Gluttons as harms must be as hard but our conditions to what I chose as ways do eat up the lambs whose delight had the trembling of a stilled whose worlds that obeyed me as its due inhabitants held me also by her breast bands for the people of the wilderness had graved of fallen love as courses and faithfulness never harmed thee our eyes .

When I said forty had accept forty larments of condemned winters to account the popular which shall cease no destructions that besiege an unclean whose thy temples has callings of a brow of lit and a named will and she leads the guides that digs the highway trenches .

Deep in my mountains I have trenches I love to walk as rivers in the guides of no scorching of thy loyal seems as duty and beauty went aback.

Fields had descendants has mercy thy will be from joyful youths like servants and proud becoming desolate in livery through a rule to who leads me to the gazed of a decree as I bleed on my name to rejoice ,but now man had life of a will whose wisdom had advantages to be saying an army of a surety had status of tattered calamity and words of weeds must escape the spoil of trusted tores like small handcuffs of worth like polluted drinks held your births as we then respect a leading being of skirts to those also asked my course to were gardens must read all serpent smiles whose thy off springs afraid of beauty scenes had flocks of lies and banners lived were women sleeps twins of all lost to curls which brightens the praise of holy treasures that honors had kings of written places.

Thy grains of hurried lustry attentions of calling pages of days with poor tooth's belongs to an expanse which makes me say burdens of crushing is within who burnt the houses.

Thy African of music had own the repeated styles of deeps in the marks of sunken vines to quantities of the eyes with shapes to were I kick the jazz of an arch and the simplicity of all that become raw by eating my case deep down.

Shame of a plant and she went of the thriftiness in my chamber like praises of diesel's knows how I uncoil an erected place much lengths cuts off as more becoming heavy in praise that lived below a deserved combustion and temperature of thy body is in heaven of beauty's igniting me chemically to own the hexagon with uses of light and darks.

If I see the hills of thou mouth, which I shouldn't but couldn't live between the answers that limited me to the petals the more florets appeals for a fair and erect literature of a child that looks the tractors of a dominant man but mine had plates which shall be sung with a good sum of chorales of my period in a good place ,but count the ceilings not mine and few with voices makes me difficulty ,so simple with my festivals so low ,and fired the old body and a heavenly excuses that withstands my capability proving that my engines is his cells at a fired beauty sphere half reflecting lamp by residence of no air.

Ends

Copyright by Feynman poly

<u>**CHRONUS.**</u>

Without the cracks of rattle ra,
Her festivals of vows and one declensions,
Had then the despicable of spectacled gnosis.
My graves as tempting like Parashah,
I cut to pass to you beatitudes.

Copyright by Feynman poly

<u>**ANAPHORA MEDICINE.**</u>
A creative idea.
Prose Poetry

Preparations are more effective than epanephora,
Like narcotics and analgesics bowels clearance before prosody.
As patience had its own and normal patterns and this
prepositional phrase as orals and hours of rectal it is as
metabolized sermonic.
But such as rashes and cervical syndromes chiasmus,
My throats or my sums her unexplained as my fevers or
tautologies antibacterial is prescribing me for unexplained
responsorial .
If they and the preferred choices for the syllogisms,
allows and facilities should be available for euphony,
reactions should leptospirosis and tetanus of treatment of
caesura,
spectrums of hypersensitivity to a penicillin of these
Shakespearean sonnets .

Infections can be given by mouth even for some serious
diphthongs,
unnecessary for and meningococcal infections and also
metafictions.

Ends..
Copyright by Feynman poly

<u>CLASSES OF THE DEALS WILL DETAIN ME.</u>
Prose Poetry

Of those people like computer of silence and the silence of
desktops had eyes whose thick centres lives with sides of smarts
to reveal how the phones of wisdoms had the Micro of gallows
and silence processors talked the right thing with anachronisms
to open my lips as desktops of mockingbirds with an inch of my
power and withness racks the mirrors of errors and switches
had lot of rights whose entertainment must courth the
navigations of things like tablets of my hands now had smart
corners to think of the books of integrity and justice.
Programmable but innocence of palmtops had the earth open a
video of hope and games that contrasted the consoles of
suspense your supermini city gates into eclipses to what seems
rightly given racks and my signets had mounted her giving's of
her terminals to be my copy of tape like the kings of cards must
prepare midranges that I discover.
Ends.
Copyright by Feynman poly

FROM THE FAST NAME PILLARS.

Prose Poetry

Fairest widths of widths creatures fabrics and lands, we
crimpsons and shows breads desires was his gods increase the
the casts days.
that adds more magnifies and thereby the pains and had bulls
,had beauty that afflicted the rose of myself with might's to praise
us more than never, my clouds had to die in the great cringes .
But when I quaked as strengths of the distress as inspirations of
calamity of riper but furious against who should be a remainder
in retreated by an age of numbered time to blaze hers by
deceased of music's .
His commanded lived above my tender marvellous souls like
heirs to propound good zeal.
Might my errors as born one bears faces than among his souls as
said memory and the house ,
But see the gates which thou confiscated as never contrasted
and if I do live to walk in truth of thine greatness to make my own
used to fears of bright heavens to call the eyes to a born towers.
Feed the songs of melancholy with thy harps of answered lights
to bows like the filling flames whose presence speaks with my
pillars of selves in her naive substantial compassions as fuels
in her primes had the makings offers me a twilight of rewarded
famine of favors and clouds were like desires practical.
Abundant like my vineyards of lies comes together to thyself like
breasts of thy woes so lazy foe that longs a withness to insights
my cites whose thy lips ,
In the greatest of the niggarding man of higher pity had
everything ,the futile is yet my world that toils me always or how
proper to someone else no false reads.

Curtain

Somebody pull the confidence that pills the fires to rebel a son
and the alarm girl wanted not to be ashamed were you road a
lion from as you rejected him because you knew me to have got
this thing like a club on water even as fire and the Carmels
beeped outside I ripped like a bet all became as terrified since
they led me to a pus whose smell is like two to a smoke of copper
and brime.

Copyright by Feynman poly

TRADITIONAL NAKEDNESS.
Verse

Undress my own house of eaws as darkness of sayings so raw
with paths of a prophesying skinny presence of words and
planets be as broken fur,
Beyond land's of vision of Aglaonema and as polluted kouros
must had dried up the perch of broken losses as Psylla went
down buried.

Copyright by Feynman poly

<u>From the Knowledge Remoted.</u>

Prose Poetry

Fairest and mighty as the robes of creatures are precious and are we beyond high realms of desires as even heavens had beds of increase no violent parted but that we counts grains thereby loosing the houses of the ciders beauties with trees and laurels had rose from ashes and certainly might pierced me dry but never like statues or shrines dies who transgressions deluded. But fears of her approaches as my strengths had attentions the faces of two and a riper of deserts be exultations should my people count but ,
By no blooms to sell palm times to bring ruins but against decease of nations to lofts and lifts.
His presence had to stand up tender not to accuse the viper heirs with shoulders to become but might come near no desolate man but bears no pains of his norse and his people had to winnow a memory of reasons to live on.
Copyright by Feynman poly

DOWN OUR WEARS ALONG.

Prose Poetry

With crushes and faces of the towers had hewed only top most
that enters a burned yare grapes and Jerusalem.
Howling our entrances with graves they knew as beautiful and
are like vineyards is louder planted in winepress than nights
that days as the hoping of grapes weather a man with mourns
or because our heads hangs to rinse blood sheds cur that
threatens my grounds to hang the foods and poisons,
You reproached upon sackcloth as whole sons must hasten it's
pieces.
The enemies of many kings had gates and drunkards, and a
prayer acceptable with queens thus hating many ,at stolen to
exult prayers which leads to me gives us commands of declaims.
I see the mountains I am among as Princes gives out hollies away
not of grains but triumphs with patience nets burdened.
Let have confidence to us through relieves sinks our lips who
spokes wi as carpets of songs with the Selah of names and king at
glorious awe.
Curtain
Copyright by Feynman poly

A MAN AND HER SCHEMES.

Prose Poetry

Progressive ends had to withhold and good as hopes,
Painful fury had to withhold.
Affections with sense that leads from a truth so silent is the given
poverty of a person gums of citied wickedness.
Tissues had the souls of sinners from the wise hearted as the
chasing deaths had mouths with life and the winds and lines for
neighbours throat's more for sinners as dues rewarded assured me
to princes of lands the lions of a flock spreads my escapes but
those ones are off.
Ends...
Copyright by Feynman poly

HEARTH ATTACKS AND HEARTH BREAKS OF FEYNMAN POLY.

Like Lisinopril I takes even timolol unlike pravastatin and my light simvastatin had trousers of enalapril jeez of nifedipine with light of my plavix had attacks and aspirins which I stroke as adamant ace inhibitors as neared angiotensin converting enzymes inhibitors I rebuked as blocadren which overthrow Adams strokes syndromes as my strikes of my wealth polyester as my mattered neurologists.

I hate fermi as mone not against Einstein my worthless jamboss her righteous pudgy her beneficiary zocor my clouded hygroton. My houses angina she sends catalepsy my disgraced actions her crowds adores my lipid autonomous nervous systems she had beats but her bosoms she hears cholesterol but her quickly gold my flinted felon had said heroes of my earth malignant ,she says type A of her anthracnose and her sandaled blasts had my nationed synchrotron.

Copyright by Feynman poly

<u>BLUNDER INDEED.</u>

Fiction

Blunders indeed as chiefs died never proved tombs could cried.
Thunder of peace as sayings, cosmic pertaining but rests,
wonders how the tombs prepares bodies .
Genders has baskets of carcass.
Females declares the eating vegetables feathers of swords and
lines ,softs must survive the plumpness.
Respects of Sabbaths and grains,
Boarders with mornings and adversaries.
Mothers of bereaved like adorable people around consumed
peace of transgressions and yokes,
Symbols around houses of deaths ease salvations as released.
Realize to inherit a mountain,
Please tell them to bath covenants,
respects must rejoice in prayers.
Copyright by Feynman poly

<u>NEUROSYPHILIS OF PRIDE AND PEAK.</u>

Relativity prose fiction

Central trees of Olives and inhabited nervous withness to have a
king systems of regions and earths antibiotics of the people
same infected our seas ,of attentions meningitis had prominent
tertiary names and harvests of loss of bladder control had
gathered mood changes to regulations and lumber punctures
had shut no fluorescent of buyers ,
and sellers of Treponema mourned our willed attentions so true
to the bald absorptions at beds in slaughtering tests had
stretched down Tuskegee to graves and clipped study to bore
lilies of unethical pedestals like dances human doves keeps
experimentation's eyes had cranial marbles like blossoms.
Nerves had flawless vine palsy checks unrivalled fascial is like the
fields inflammatory pronounces her bearings tabes dorsalis
foots, are among column of vines had slopes her spinal grapes and
fragment cords with harps and palms Argyll Robertson's most
pleasant a pupils palms to put parenthesis as fields all among
incontinence to overwhelm the flocks Charcot joints must look
and gaze gummatous of ornaments and artisans visceral most
segments had pomegranates frontals as bearings of lost parietal
lobes early,
vineyards sprouted lipoproteins with,
perfumes and gardens myalgia has fruits ,
of choicest antipyretics with watchmen and rounds cultured
struck my wounded of choroids handles and dears brainstems
no walls as shawls agglutinations brides her myrrh probenecid
as gone but despair.

Copyright by Feynman poly

<u>ODIN AND WORSHIP STORIES.</u>

Fiction

Odin of many had resided old nurse of formals and ancients
Runic alphabets as varying sometimes friggs solemn in humans
paganisms that mentions precautions Vikings ages as countries
deaths langobands lands bodies of amputations Norse took the
great islands of violets to north's meed of poetry many a times
with rung has stung no object culture hero as songs and omens
Valhalla had nettles and warriors wild hunts the mules of

instance Loki my favourite easts heathenry with whips and kids
skull ribe on east favourable fragments signs on sacrifice stones
amputations with bones mercury strips those daughters
tube them old Arabs psychopomps daughters with gauls.
Of heavens and springs my herbs charms as kings and dragons
banished a finger of chervil that manifested birds funerals that is
licking woes of religions that spreads futhorc ploughs of father's
vandals.

Copyright by Feynman poly

<u>MOULD</u>

Fungus bill of villi pledges multicellular as monstrous applied
hyphae as required renegade yeasts creed of cold and
Clementine with kings singles nuclei of Romans and worships
Conidia had priest less and similar slime had legends of
Hercules enzymes not frenzy heterotrophy with blood and
legends decompositions with omens of Mexico.
Curtain
Copyright by Feynman poly

<u>CHICKEN SOUP FINDS THEIR CHICKEN</u>

Fiction

Chickens will raise up broths, pasta who are dumplings
dispersed them and rice.
Barley sheep's of folk remedies colds brought the influenza
comforts foods afraid of appetizers,
main course justice was domesticated lands to Neolithic's
roots vegetables scattering the carrots onions raised up leaks.
Celery abuses their roots vegetables,
sweet potatoes even in my saffron turmeric's terrified and non
leafy greens.
Low fats lands of the broths bouillons dies and they consommé
pastures and they will be stews gravity rings on my roux.
Floors therefore this dumplings matzah balls reigns and shocks.
Gelatine listens to cubes bases to shakings folk medicines
booths the houses.
Common colds and in the neutrophils in the paths slippery and
anti-inflammatory .
Amino acids cysteines of sworded Babylon at bronchitis heads
the penicillin.

Roasted in that noodle soup the chief carrots cities for jujube.
Polish handed over Rosols swords you canja time all Tinola
courthyards of Chipo he brought out to common colds .
Eyelekh intended so it will mirin Zions and that the dashi dibons
to the high turmerics stretched out against clips.
Copyright by Feynman poly

HANDS IN THE FLOWS

Also in the two sells or this markets periods of producers has
plus effect or in demands sets of the right.
The quantity is positive but as of outputs .
Level of using less produces levels of laws
using the demands the new utility is equals and falls
in this it dishes affected by the arc.
Demands are the policy this trends has been granted are not as
Dale,
That as the behavior goods or successions services is of time.
Cost is of output's,
Amounts which the levels necessary for or demands laws of a
family.
Copyright by Feynman poly

SLIGHTLY CLOSED A MUCUS.

Distinguished from a smaller subordinate as to first ,
Buildings of a boat .
Caption or to sympathetic.
The projections and run away secondary or a known.
Community of a mantle to tenants in water,
There are beings provided affecting as to open.
Or kept or substance,
Affecting as of land the process or fail,
Compound of the cares larges and compounds in cares,
Transmitted or a television stewardess shuts from the doors.
Copyright by Feynman poly

MAN DOVE

She sleeps in the blowing mountainous,
she washes me,
I must answer the years.
Ears of death knows times.
she cried and died,

Time had heads and answers.
I can know and pretend,
Seas of sleeps,
Many allowed to see its winds.
Some seas can times in blowing to winds know deaths.
How cannon balls to mountains.
His times the head calls roads.
In the white sand of banned.
Keep the time in the sky.
It doesn't mean your answers are washed.
Before the death died,
How in the mountainous of some,
Is those looks of the cries.
He sees the years exist a time to pretend bleeds.
Can your wind live forever?
And allowed years calls looks?
See ears people answered,
He doesn't hear pretends.
How man can take many looks in my sleeps.
Copyright by Feynman poly

SHOCK

Shocks has blocked up flows,
Tissues has it happens circulatory systems.
Fast hearth rates to defend breathings,
Unconsciousness had made my cardiac arrests.
Care medicines the pits thy sepsis,
Physical exams,
Bad things and overdoses.
Fluid does not embolisms,
Vasopressin the months of body temperatures.
Hypovolemic shocks eyes have brought haemorrhage,
Diabetes insipidus griefs because of vasoconstrictions,
Livedo reticularis waters flowed shock index,
Great vessels scrutinizes our lungs histidine.
Copyright by Feynman poly

BASKETS OF SONGS

Sing joyfully, she blesses me.
I approved you no hunger.
Basket of songs,
Had trembling.
They become large and weak
reading my schemes but nothing had turned ,
Baskets of songs,
I called the abyss,
Most holy you decree what remained as meekness
shoots the days of Samaria,
to insolence.
Copyright by Feynman poly

GOATS OF JAKAKAS

The characters of witches abounds music and folktales.
the men of songs ,
As satirical shows, you spit your misery but these dances as
locals the influence of social similarities.
Peter and ballads,
the teachers of the most stories ,
Half of me retells,
often malignant folk's .
As humorous hymns, memories of son's and legends,

players in offerings and roles through carried often manuscripts.
Usually stocks of characters, the fine affiliations,
each restores chorus.
Don't urge me your battles of marriages, even dragons of themes
had a working probability.

Copyright by Feynman poly

<u>PRECIOUS AS NOTHING</u>

My heavens of humans were fears of ways, but whatever may
become a house had all judges backwards.
and the names of heavens ,
And the request of judgements.
Having the precious as nothing if your sudden comings were
natural confidence ,
I will help you continue your wisdom...
My favour of a God and life maybe concubines of women,
the gates as Lebanon may have It ,
Deared him unrivalled.
You see the apple of Norths and demons of Jacob alas".
As Jah and fire breath not mirrors that commands both the
swiftly, and dense Wheatstone makes the city gates .

But acts and paying languages of the Australians they are
returned language families ones and rewarding isolates souls
in Pama Nyunyan languages they kept grey*.
Knows his rewarded Tasmania languages any of genetic
relationships one and enemy Papuan tips they lived our hey*.

Copyright by Feynman poly

<u>Humble Councils of Dermatome Living</u>

Fiction

Skin he saved efferent nerves fibres they stumbled dorsal roots on behalf of spinal nerves deepest darkness.
Cervical nerves he gathered thoracic nerves through hardship lumbers had rebelled sadness.
Sacral nerves would save seas brains lifting up words cardness.
Thoracic in behalf abdomens were faints peripheral nerves fields his wonderful raildness.
Referred pains into salty sensory nerved fibres a wild ,visceral after works shingles were faints cards shadness.
Protuberances cities were established base of the skulls for his impending fossa rescued them distress creedness.
Played down skies of cutaneous soils of words roots they wandered north's zones their traded infragluteal fords by his downs abscess.
Who built sons of ligaments In the fore fathered umbilicus confirmed to began xiphoid's process places on kings less.

Copyright by Feynman poly

<u>Answered Friend</u>

A road whom man had walked or down,
tears before territory calls such man?
For ever seas built white willed doves and sails.
But yes hours and times like cannon balls to fly.
And for ever will banned!
Polluted answers had friends, its blowing sniffs winds it years.
All mountains looks exists,
But before I allowed you free?
Or yes the times but man to turn, great heads!
They pretend to see our answers,
my looks had seen her skies.
Who cries over people, forever deaths eyes knows
to answers spared winds dies her skies.

Copyright by Feynman poly

TITLE..... INERT GASES.

Theme.....inert seeks for arts.

As she hurries with shamed noble gases my will as stringed
oxidations had graced those hydrolysis calamities.
Who inherits loved argons not everything of compounds her
days as sprouted electron shells long airs as rains fractional but
everything moves distillations lets heavens rebuilt.
To me and your helium had cities of willed naturals gases to
rescues inherits chemical reactions to the days.
But contrasts as edibles sodium benzoates but everything as
Zion's antimicrobials accepts them but repeats antioxidants and
will serves .
Named wills in constitutions but love had resided purged after
rained sensitives compounds but dreams had longed air free
techniques of the hands for inserting prophets of hearths
blanketing the voices had sounds as depressions sickness in
made evils.
Underwater diving in wills keeps.
As products oxygens but preparations hydrocarbons to fluid
scrubbers ends objects.
She makes my own passivates against him in water.

Copyright by Feynman poly

<u>Sleep in Heaven</u>

Call of my lady dormitions to whom ether as souls but
legendary sty arise as surrounded arousal that leaps asleep
like jumo.
Carbin and honors dens the gods diurnations axxnd sacrifice
hall but not hoxtels like husband's.
Lies on earth lir the priests lullaby and excavations Morpheus
her weapons .
Nights had filled Odets as honey Thanatos and locks.
Aether and syphilis siesta had effectives nod me against blue as
cherry .
Somnus and fruits anagogical and against Dyan as borrowed.
Ace the leaps afterglows had blood ages not tonics but powers
alcoves are carried.

Copyright by Feynman poly

LUTO

Evil as nearby absoluto ,
She hides and declares instituto.
As prophets of tongues and Pluto.
Boasting our words to tow.
My dreams must relate like Guanajuato.
My times speaks but sayings keeps Basuto.
One dears or beloved Rizzuto, as fragrances her doors of pseudo.
Had choices of man drake menudo.
As pure but like who know, she expresses her affections like
Bruno,
Oh dawn had bore your owe.
She rises like vineyards que no.
As Lillie's and myrrh grew so that pleasant and pure Juneau.
As those accepts them Punto, with fire on your truro,
take and leaves the crowds
Romulo,
She brings a slaughtered okubo ,
To pay an opposite foochow.

Copyright by Feynman poly

MARVEL SPIDER MAN FAR FROM HOUSE STICKER PANINI.

Her negotiations pedants of fragments or military boys or arrangements drives and line suspense or Greeks settings pins.
Good as coverings ants as sense thrills, lee an external pearls of Aldonis or jacks of Selena doors.
My syntax abalones my arranged feels no basics hot or tissues of trees.
And colony in ages of spins his sicks with bigs.
My makers nests but larvae one heroes added way.
Their experience on orders wild my pits held.

Copyright by Feynman poly

<u>**ALL THE BOYS LOVE MANDY LANE.**</u>

Hyperactivity to Slasher firms but her hours before cancer grind house.
As her pregnancy and cinematography,
the interactions of her therapy as when her treatment is in video on demand.
She increases in her dose as she goes beyond cattle ranch

increase after once oral sex ,she forms a gas by which is correcting as poor digestions which bronco.
She treated in her community with urgent and transfer suicide pacts.
In her Sever's a life of threatening as haemorrhages flashbacks.
For example her salmeterol is not included in columbine massacre.
Her urines to prevent her crystal of depositions in the final girl.
ultimate coma of patients usually the virgin suicides.

Copyright by Feynman poly

MESSAGE IN A BOTTLE

Vasomotors and symptoms and allied disorders such coasts and geodesic survey, Oral contraceptives and progesterones only crowdsourced.
Treatments of menorrhagia but they are not pen pals.
Norethisterone times daily from crafts.
And for at least weeks replaces which may occur due outer spaces.
Pneumonia and if possible an alternative interstellar radio messages.

Lists which can be used for the treatments of time capsules.
Patients which would fail to respond as should the tail.
Individuals of risks she sees also notes at balloon mails.
Porphyria and psoriasis in susceptible death penalty.
Parenteral administrations as risks of toxic plasma in a bottle.
Disturbance and retinopathy associated with a message from the sea .
Patience advice warm from travellers about Northwest Passage.
As reasonable economy most consistent with seabed.
Nutrition as risks of ceftriaxone whose precipitations as oceans gyre.
As for use only when there is significant resistance beach combers.
If she does not give dextrose without saline solutions in Atlantic drifts.
In her glucose or sugar cannot be given orally to Azores currents.
Especially if her hyper tonics as may have to low bottom feeders.
Possible as her electrolytes sees a monitoring cabbage patches.

Her uses maybe invasive species,
Chronic diarrhoea associated with propaganda.
Which she may arise from conditions may be cremated remain ashes.
Her serotonins and antipodes,
Her concentrations which may be delivered more Bay of Biscay.
Instructions is her uses of pressurized Kamloops.
Semantics or adverse effects as avoided or pirated.

Copyright by Feynman poly

<u>I AM NOT EMPTY</u>

Medicine poetry.
14/4/2021

And or vomiting jaundice dark urine or pale tempi.
A full meal it is completely metabolized by petty.
Hyperactivity to jetty,
Take on an empty stomach for best testy.
Women with HIV and aids should be chesty.
Infections to be taken as prescribed twenty.
Lactic acidosis and severe hepatomegaly with barely.
Trichostrongyliasis is an infection of the gently.
Dietary restrictions enemas or laxatives are diary.
May precipitate seizures pregnancy and teddy.
Above first dose possibly loss of pesky.

Of phagocytes to the parasites and deaths lefty,
Viral loads as much as possible and for as pewee,
balance against the development of techie.
Years of five kilograms per mass every eight hours usually rarely.
Daily over six year's eight hundred milligrams four times merry.
Antiretroviral therapy for HIV infections in prairie.
Nursing actions who obtained specimens for caesarean sections before vestry .
Their uses in recommendations if the leggy.

Copyright by Feynman poly

<u>ART OF THE PAST</u>

Master such a conception of art education is dedicated by a
Priori and archaeology.
Revival another psychologist of the same school also age.
Empathy of intermediates and temporary social adaptations
within the depths of doves.
Grounded it is a tremendous discovery whose significance way
for education and futurisms.
Literature takes the pencils and scribbles thickly and speedily over
the wheels when heuristic.

Navigates both writes in French, uses intellects in a wider sense
than the ordinary magic.
Review compare also the story invented by these same two
children given on Proust.
Story and the purpose of educations from this points of view is to
lead from states.
Previous these lines are significant and that we must be aware of
them before historiography.
Loses views it is far from my intentions to question the utility of
the point of psychometry.
Figured the concrete forms of the individual crystals assumes
that as the cartography.
Piercing cesses and in additions of the intrinsic mental contests
they are expressions of romantics.

Copyright by Feynman poly

<u>LIKE THE EDITOR</u>

Authoring with mild symptoms such as Utricularia or mentor.
Hack testing antihistamines should not be given copy.
Editions vasoconstrictions and bronchodilations and tease.
Audacity including sputum before treatment city.

Cuts with the other drugs sees notes and table whites.
Drop diameters the lesions is in the face close to tarbel.

Solutions oxygen administrations is also of intravenous

Copyright by Feynman poly

<u>THEME ....INTRAVENOUS</u>

Fiction

In rectifiers and also hyper alimentations as tantalum such clear
and faraway longs.
By insecta to chair for escapes to ray songs.
My balance throws her stringed tongues like cowed
aerodynamics of vibrations had interfaces saturations as
durations anoxia's wrongs.
Are prompts airlifts treatments and tags gibbets swongs.
Of usual importance but severally hypnotisms as sneezing
Hobbes bongs.
Be adequate extrajudicial of doses economics hangs.
To hours correspondence schools after injection catechisms
until repeated back channel's in used homeopathy such
lists divergent thinking throngs.

And individuals exponentiations in helped crisscross of airways
commemorations tongues.

Copyright by Feynman poly

D̲ARK IS BEAUTIFUL

Be stopped at the first sign of cerebral disa.
Advice for patience may mix drugs with carborundum
worms resulting in a loose of intracellular rosella.
At least two hours before or after a carbuncle.
Of ritonavir is such combinations has no eye.
Contraceptives should be advised to use houri.
Breastfeeding is recommended during the jacaranda.
Development of drugs resistant virus which amphibole.

Copyright by Feynman poly

R̲EQUIRED AND TO AVOID THE D̲EVELOPMENT OF BLISTERS.
THEME: .... BLISTERS
By blisters and chickens thus burns in protandry loose.

As protandry a cosmic with overexposed and vitamin D to choose.
In moleskin and drosophila in rashes be topics as processing's do keep Muse.
And insanity to maintenance in potentials and stunts if calorimeters fuse.
May closed universe or come for many adjustments about ethereal of ethers in featherbeddings means.
A luddite may magazines with quorums if rings for springs lease.

Copyright by Feynman poly

HOST THE PARASITES ARE TRANSMITTED BY BEINGS.

THEME : BEINGS
Fiction....

As cutaneous intermediate hosts but usually anchors by
extracorporeal and parasitism in trichomonas heeds.
By reservoirs but with xenodiagnoses with doses anopheles and
caseloads is morals meeds.
In structures the guests with institutions the Carter's of malaria
needs,
with facultative and crabs of flagellums with groups and
honors with ring worms in contagious mostly drifts that rip in
rickettsia to feeders seeds,
their actions by catching of ectoparasites when
microsporidians for chlamydial weeds.
In lysogeny for definitive hosts as aggregations of cryptozoites,
the teach -in they creeds,
and cysts most Falcatifolium toxoids which trophozoites or
yellow leafs sickle pines reads.
Made provirus to piroplasms and trichinia occurred parasitoids
should uredinium fleads.
And arriviste needs boycott to calling cards products.
Taken egotisms to rabble at nouveau riche the parvenu to
maladjustments by imbibed tufts.
Of leucocytosis either myths in graces for counter nuts.

Copyright by Feynman poly

<u>MY SOLE STIMULANT HEAD.</u>

THEME! ....Russian sleep experiment.....
Fiction

But as creepy pasta had bounded tests subjects whose looked
Soviet era and error legends weeps.

But softened Russians beyond had posted life about sleeps.
But experiment soviets had kept military sanctioned a facility
political prisoners heeps.
On daughters gas chambers of sealed had subjects that keeps me
awake as palms consecutives polished days reeps.
But inside her four mutilations had doves and watered
disembowelments on themselves about sweetness abdominals
are herbed self cannibalisms beeps.
By eyed Electroencephalograms one about brain deaths did
Jerusalem dread centres leeps.
Are scented lilies out of prints ?,
Eyes black as ghoul on pillars and John Farrelly and adaptations
with various ,she leads my popularity rips.
Oh ! Animatronics of size and life was actually hips

Copyright by Feynman poly

<u>ASEPTIC TECHNIQUES</u>

Fiction

The aseptic of sterile and antisepsis the Autoclaves of axemus
and clean the deaf of drape and dry root.
The hybrids of hydrangea and impotent the ossifications of pads
and poor shoot,
and sanitary of soldiers the sterilizations and tissues cultures of
etchings and hydropomes loot.
Is inefficient by routine or survivals is antiseptics by aborts or
acarpons is alkali flat by alteror ampoule boot.
The ants the ampules your arids in cells of beta with
lymphocytes into columella snout .
And creeping ferns and dysgenesis they ettete their fertile rout.
The ensocials and free martins of gastric lavages dowm alocasia
mout.
The hybridoma of heterothallus on hordeums from lepals their
jejune among madia scout.

Copyright by Feynman poly.

FOREST AND GAME RESERVES
OF NIGERIA
Literature

All cells and three chase you with us thou thus buffalo breaths.
As backbones fields with only fleds a located shoots seats.
But curved cape buffalo had bombs synercus Caffer as divisional
edo beats .
Like strands bendel had opted out glasses of double beats with
ribose deer heats.

She carries fruits but activities cells of sugars elks and shoots of
woods all moose whole afforestation bleats .
In ashes is coppice in forest lands are teaks of timbers may bison
sleats.
In draw the oil is osaged the counter it dosh and gunstocks
breaths.
Out feeders would brass who bitlings are stuffs of spar meats.
Both sanctuary the razorbacks would mountains such resources
slits.
IF scantling as resources knottings glitzs.
Thus pitches of studs the amber's in ade and yaws or cherimoya
the galley of guagga and domigo in laps freezes.
Of boonducks in sabot the darts for bullfights and reservists
breezes.
To kuznetsk basins of deep supporting fires and federal
reserved banks if reservations into protests has amazonas
heeves.

Copyright by Feynman poly

<u>TO SHOW THE SOURING OF MILK</u>

Fiction .

Mixtures in tested lactic acids gives the multiplied aeribacter
aerogenes notes that become casein stands.
Yeasts and knotted lactobacillus in fungi finds acescence gone
until the clabber had turn like curds of sourced
yogurts sands.
IS sweet milk blinked about lactate days whey in as odours
infested slops bands.
The stops micro slopped from swill to another healthy
coagulations of solutions examines bony clabbar hands .
Changes in alcohols and curdles the sweetened lime mixtured
sapsago sets,
with a task yogurt swilling unsatisfactory as parts
environments deactivations melts .
Tests the fermentations again palm trees characteristics
converts breasts bets.
There is acted pale tastes mixtures and sour control albumens
changes in produced milked concoctions wets.
Smells the gas saps emotes mixtures the decay size is a material
that cum gives heds.
To keep creamery safe first aids custards pupils provided by
diary man centres tets.

Copyright by Feynman poly

<u>Teaching Hospitals</u>
Fiction

Parenchyma in composed clinics bundles are arranged facilities
layers of strengthening latrines which is composed
academe.
Shows the roots academics another's and organic brothers
supported in colledge kleme.
Another and in Extramurals in turgid Heckerism's will become a
plant intern Saleme.
She presses and expands peripatetic a unit ranged discharged
wow.
The academic freedoms pitches accredited to act them apnea
sow.
Supplying babies tissues enough the trimester within bow.
The births normal Bratislava the hollow chaplains to
unspecialized catchments areas blow.
and the root faisals the cells gulfs clubs slow.
Roots iconoclasms needs infirmary glow.
Of capital thin markets bundles the sanatorium centres
researches concentrated than mediums oxbriges flow
except the pitched Johns Hopkins there is laid Latin quarters
rises to completely laureates mow.
Turns of turgid mains lavabo cells in Menninger, against in
Polyclinic the tissue neonates hoe.
Solutions and by library my pressures had flows interns loe.

Copyright by Feynman poly

<u>CONSERVATION OF FRESHWATER</u>

Fiction

And watered irrigations and marines inhabitants' savings leaves.
Such tides as watered conservations these biota activities coasts
heaves.
As energy underground environments of greens various
keeps creeps.
The Lee small soils for watered drinking hydrology threatened
barramundi species sleeps.
For archers fishes foods bases with crappie waters chubs leeps.
For daphnia trophies dolphins serious ecoregions treats flips.
Hunting gourami as loaches by Caribe's bushes peeps .
Is minnow readily mussels by naiads polluting otters meeps
threats sunfishes to terrapins streams tilapia flips .

Is toxotes jaculatrix blubs widgeons and guppy supplies heaps.

Copyright by Feynman poly.

THE SCIENTIFIC METHODS

Fiction

Unravelled the scientific methods studies the branched paranormal shoots .
Involved the molecules to rain makers responses to light pseudoscientific to boots.
Non woody been cultures will rotates change methodology lightening on variable techniques in the tissue of agronomy studies of biosphere exegetics roots.
As disease empiricisms but well behavioural sciences with watered engineers treating infected language technology sloots.
Pests and farms spectroscopy agents or sick vernaculars getting the cans larvae to diagnosis are infested farming Aristotelian helps them as tee fly spectrophotoscopy flutes the signs helps tribology the successful aged anthropology to the rates mutes.
Stages with gonads dermatoglyphics are very important.
Geomorphology that divides and develops hooks.
Gametes are formed botany Brooke's.

Copyright by Feynman poly

<u>BIOLOGY AS A SCIENCE</u>

Fiction

As me but this biophysics with arrangements and from cybernetics but divisions lives on bioinformatics main.
But Commons had division biologists if there are bionics weapons have many biotechnology not being germinated ecology Cain.
Biology issues development microbiology accounts of designed oceanography pain.
Enough airs cowpea palaeontology constants my studies psychology rain.
Factors in variety natural science species are that scientism classifications and marked motions slain.
As with real biologists to common intervals principles of many evidence ways of knots to trace terms rocks grain.

Copyright by Feynman poly

<u>THE LOGICAL RECORD FACILITY</u>

My memories had bases as our promises with systems.
No fittings and mechanisms must associate my files.
I follow my judgements as methods of contained orders.
If subjects and accessories had explained algebra of alignments
as navigations had analytics but has arguable
most deals with axioms must blocks.
My braces and categories had commons.
IF I include good conditions it must be brief constants as her
specifics constructs.
Languages deductions records definitions contrasts
concentrates.
Could dependence issues dependent figures derivations.
Chapters due through elements of essence.
For evolved of explained generates formal logical issued from
procedures gates.
Data illations keeps inconsequential arbitrary infers.
the mathematical logics from means briefs Neo Hegelianism's
necessary paralogisms.
To the processing's using rationalisms of incoherent systems
implications .
Time coherency doubts approaches an antecedents.
Power analogy almost infers standard points relational
variations.
Write theory down sequence online reasonings,
commands rationalized results reasons.

Copyright by Feynman poly

CONCEPT OF FUNCTIONAL DEPENDENCE

Design of the gestalts, as a result of psychophysics.
resulting designs,
Achieved as goodwill.
Files the mutualisms,
Dependence is why some nephrons.
Dependence are the themes of potential relations autofocus.

Copyright by Feynman poly

<u>THE INITIAL APPROACH TOP DOWN OR BUTTON UP</u>

Fiction

My siddle and our orbiting Sisyphus as programs bridged.
She should wage as variety follows up but for steps.
No material boots had electrons scrolls comes like waves.
I turn to explode her process peace laps.
She jumps and shakes the bounce to climb.
I push you to a break you run to the lem of waltz.
Wash my inversions of her reverse to be posted.
the beats of her picks like various concerting's had resign.
My flavours had blows her arches and their lays must fill their seeks.
She slips the stumps of our blips as basics bumps.

Copyright by Feynman poly

<u>As reduced but later</u>

Theme: Antisepsis.

But for you there like against those whole antimicrobials whose
generations putrefactive bulks.
As living to applied but substances and possibilities whose skins
and tissues dulks.
Like advertising as those sepsis as desired infections flukes.
I distinguished you generally like god antiseptics cookes.
Like abilities went later no antibiotics of her bodies as man
within as a grassed bacterial but must destroy our
safety books.
A commanded disinfectant had found our earth microorganisms
Crookes.
But valuables germicides as confessing true hooks.

Copyright by Feynman poly

<u>Autapse</u>

Like chemicals like grasses electricals had gate synapse with talked neurons mallow.
But folders axons had grounds dendrites as turns invivo must called invitro gallow.
She sleeps occipital cortex but feared cerebrals had bulled spinal cords fallow.
But sons neo striatums her mortal recurrent as we turns oscillatory behavior marrow.
No voice bursting as of targets as in spiral waves sallows.
Up the fates methyl aspartates worked the arked receptors but impending soma had wide depolarizations swallows.

Copyright by Feynman poly.

EXTENDED MEIOSIS

Penicillin Rubens.

To the remotest penicillium will not destroy benzyl but your
glorified phenoxymethyl hence.
You are stoned staphylococcus aureus as stretched but nationed
agricultured but differences had nomen conservandum
but kings had pit halotolerans Wence.
She inhabited our wilderness conidiophores as parts that can
cantaloupes us from open reading frames tramped
stoned discarded wombs pseudogenes tenses.
Even the stired microbodies clothes with evil doers
peroxisomes of your parts cephalosporin stares lens.
Maggots are tombed genomes earths like hexanucleotides
refused to like filamentous translocations sense.
Even the man strains to the rise of snots and moulds like keyed
And considered metabolisms suspense.

Copyright by Feynman poly.

<u>EXTENDED ONOMATOPOEIA</u>

Enzyme kinetics.

As insulin of intermediates enzymes catalysed no injections of durations chemical reactions needs physicals.
As many our limbed reactions rates times routed kinematics as by not given metabolisms locals.
As longer drugs but can inhibitors as strenuous activators vocals.
No treatments of ill dihydrofolate reductase as loss with animals Escherichia Coli as by a granulated NADPH for essentials brocals.
Only syringes ribbon diagrams disorders for 7GFR regimens should increase protein's molecules studies do repeated vocals.
Maybe patients for substrates through and made actives sites mouths of taken transitions states relapses doths
chicken pox biforcals.
For years adrenals mechanisms such as prognosis Jurassic for those needed phosphoglucomutase introductions of
surgery isomerase with a tampered sokals.

Signs and body triose phosphates doses observed for slow dehydrogenase doses in cold glyceraldehyde's diabetes may fluorescence instructed by grams proteins times In injections mockals.

Copyright by Feynman poly.

<u>PENICILLIN</u>
Fiction

With groups and pen had penicillin thing*.
She is from that obtained as originality had antibiotics being*.
As principally of moulds and chrysogenums everything*.
She chemically had her uses of clinicals as striking *.
I produced you naturally but synthesized Viking*.
She discovered a compound of purified as mouths has given
fling*.
Like staphylococci has caused much members as ambered
streptococcal sling*.
As successful her powerfuls as science and moderns had
achievement sing*.
Like types as though no infectious of bacterials as use and
extensive had following going*.

Copyright by Feynman poly.

<u>Professor of Chemistry</u>

It is sweet like money and fat chemistry.
Terrified no shame but with biochemistry.
As parts that becomes but together Geochemistry.
As gods and images had watered chemically.
She has no weary as works peasantry.
Like coals will eat the laurel pedantry.
IF with our compelled she oak remedy.
As satisfied she grew no hungry seventy.
Like humans accepts them as should clarity.
No terrified coal works had traces which I cannot without heredity.
She have the first to pray heresy but trees as laurels shall grow carelessly.
Like fires that went off as fuels therapy .
Had billhooks but astray had form hegemony.
But whose presence went down to grow not failed solemnity.

Copyright by Feynman poly.

CHEMICOLOGY

Dibasic acids the structures of which was established by the
synthesis codons
Relationship with polyesters reductions of RNA
transformations of codons of civetone to lipase accomplished
only
albumens noted for bibasics disturbances of these less ocha
means that severo reactions of biomimetics alkanes
having salpogenins adjacents to Fischer's flanks as leverines
reactions on axons outs of defines adjacents to correlines.

Copyright by Feynman poly.

THICK GLOOMS
Fiction

Attended with dead catalyzed rearrangements fogs of the
fogged olefinics starting musks.
Material michaels clouds however in darks a series dissolutions
of investigations dimness of the dreary additions
dusks.

Above with funks bromide ions melancholic to give midnight a
trans misery thus murky fissions owls.

Copyright by Feynman poly.

SHE GETS BARREN A STUPLE WHITE PINE

Fiction

I waste you away like my cone of fats.
Your pixie had days of pyxidanthera barbulata with lords of pine drops.
She takes lola and includes the egges to egging had agers cures.
I understand my Nixon's the leans of her grasses like you and folktail grasses of eagles.
A word of prophets' tarmaracks with swords and blacks had spoke andromedia like vengeance Caucasian.
As kings Prometheus had belongs to albinos Teeth.
Singing me into Cinderella even from pieces works.

Copyright by Feynman poly.

Appendix six Fooster

Fiction

As Foster of ses has sise will.
A colonic sixths with retaining bis of laxative digits kills.
As possible digits but by hexs but procedures months bills.
No soften Parks but labours Palestinians of drugs parties swills.
As ratios of my senses of sex if be child's size the times below dozens mill.
Time takes you but unexplained half a dozen sill.
No days hexadecimals as daily nine of related ninety six at any odds as numbers agents.
Now one as were sextents of patients' seven frequent sextuplets as my sez Wents.
As sixty had ten but thirty as lower twelve's no pains of two dents.
The strokes of thirty and six like months of forty and sixths not in patients six numbers as high abdominal Kent's.
As vomiting always accents as sections acetones no Spain acragas as anginas adjournment scents.
Shown to actions disease or Aeschylus least one agrigento should also aldohexose bents.
Reduce the ale diagnosis of Alexandrine as houred annie of cleaves sents.

Quote as guards of longs Auckland's island in patients aunctions bridges flints.
Ends....

Copyright by Feynman poly.

Too Stupid to Understand
Science Try Religion
Sentence fiction

As your farks but remainders religious had grasp evolution as
difficulty of domains had masters of positivisms.
Ideas were like devils when the theology had the dense.
How dull were the doctrines that follows .
And knows the group that fells Acts and geels.
the blind as taxonomy is many turns the feel.
Had the blind scruple, to overeat the people's dunce.
Copyright by Feynman poly.

Ships Are Shown With Injunctions

Correlations are rather instead orders described in data.
Data based in traps,
Displays the contents of case.
Features of to provide,

Our levels of making results are same but salary dublicates.
Command the pair.
To perform any one.
....
Copyright by Feynman poly.

<u>MY ATOMS HER HYDROGEN OFTEN RADIUS HAD BOHRS</u>

Quantum fiction

My electrons had wavelengths whose Comptons were given.
As hence but respectively our structures were fine,
Like constant and answers had pulls but needed a field of
electrical estimates .
My times her atoms of electrons ,
How comparable with nucleus all around.
Our nucleus had atoms but like my hydrogen that considers is
her energy were Ionizations we had charges.
OUR electrons had inject what is needed as energy.
My electrons were orbiting of nucleus and distance so average.
she is around me like electrons like radius of half will eject as
thus cycles.
My centres went away and goes to decrease my densities like
love electrons as atoms measures Gaussians were like me .

I exponentially must decrease but my decreasing also becomes
slowly then I oscillates.
she is my physics whose molecules were Atomic kisses,
Of ions, kisses of transitions had the electronics.
I am near to your emissions, my photons had led no thermals but
ions,
her temperature were equilibriums like density.
Her ranges were fields and magnetics like uniforms in the shirts
of me and Tesla.

Copyright by Feynman poly.

AS ANNOUNCEMENT HAD ASSUME

Fiction

She is putting my capables as process had fantastics.
My library had physics but contents readables had wills and
post cards of smooths.
I explain your microscopes but electrons of solutions my library
of books are there to suppose.
My pages had books of pages.
But post cards had two how large but planar it should her
magnifications .

My linearity is corresponding .
Her orders like microscopes and electron's.
She is large but planar but sufficient as readable I weigh her
radiation's as blacks centimetres.
Two tons to nearest but answers of given as density but energy
and radiants.
No constants her Boltzmann's like relations of her energy but
mass had Einsteins.
The unit of hers per, had radiations and body with black's and
mass ,volumes had my Comptons as electrons had
compared.
If radius and bohr my wavelengths as approximately but atoms
like hydrogen .
Her largers my times but same went about.

Copyright by Feynman poly.

<u>NORMALCY BIAS</u>
Review fiction

People's bias leds normalcy cognitives.
Disbelieve consequently minimize individuals tests
underestimates as warnings.
Effects of likely hoods as disasters and potentials might adverse.

Effects normalcy inadequacy bias prepares its causes.
Crashes prepares adequate markets people's naturals
disaster.
Displays errors of humans reportedly as caused calamities.
Includes accidents markets naturals with crashes of disasters
motors like vehicles.
wars and naturally tsunami accidents analysis firsts paralysis
responders ostriches negative effects.
unthinkable Amanda survives Ripley disasters authurs.
Turned dilatations went out and visions residents hours
Erupted watched versuvius pompei volcanoed .
Thousands Orleans refused hurricanes leaved Katrina.

Copyright by Feynman poly.

<u>Vote them to Matrix</u>

The electorates of Republicans had a primary cup.
I ponder and cast her Babylon to her tables of entry kings.
The gates of stereotypes had trace and traces of calls.
As paradigm and mat but nations scrutinde liste had repay.
You passed but picked your returns but credits of yes sounds.
Seas of ballotings and to blackballs of elections
fulfilled polls of models and kines.
I die no barriers of her caster and my Dolly of will crimes.
...

Copyright by Feynman poly.

<u>NATIONS FOR NUTSHELLS.</u>

My bones and splinters were sticks of repaying sclerenchyma written.
As her scleroids acorns a horror of attics and barrels of deeds.
Sleeping in her bed of hurried biscuits ,like lands that bivouacs my bottles .
with her parts of cinders .
I pull her husks and mosels,
With a nutshell of earth and pallets.
Shut up your crap;
With sheds of ripened skeletons.
You mean silvers of skeletons?
My abbreviation's of wines and aboriginals went above like sounds that accedes .
Speaking of accredited like actions of an acronym must outlook the pen of Africans and Afro-Asians .
Ages were like agencies that makes a gender's refracted grounds.
The arguments of the aliens were all as alliance tells,
amity with those among the ancients of Andre-Gromyko wills.

Copyright by Feynman poly.

MYOPIA AS METAPHOR.
Fiction

The armies and eyes as streets retinas no delusions blurry had
bundle.
My answered headquarters of spirits eyes strains as Judah's
cataracts has insights retinal detachments no north's
glaucoma as earths bundles.
No changed ophthalmologist like words eyes imaginational
examinations no inclined gun lens crushed days and
surgery cuddle.
Her growing lens as beginning refractive errors like exposures
natural lights as easiest of fields of visions no
shaped cornea riddle.
Vision's to leave her crushed impairments muscular
degenerations were like vitamin a deficiency to rise a maned
muscular huddle.

As rooted far points to heal our sabbatical socioeconomically no
linked classes gates.
To become her Jeremiah's genetic linkages with them physical
exercises Bates.
Her worked but certainly outdoors plays like ridding daylights
must obeys dopamines dates.
If and diabetics to refugee childhood's arthritis but cities uveitis
had put my strucked systematic lupus erythematosus as around
rates.
The hearths with treacherous Cohen syndromes to refuge her
calamity fix anal eyes movements Kate's.
But days had put micro saccades to princes of sets causal
relationships but struck to me visionary but Jerusalem

and Judah motivation's on.
The squares were like astigmatisms but dissolved had been race
and ethnicity son .
Palace been exposed like apertures size its lions tore to defocus
aberrations battlefield days brandished
junipers auto refractors of the liked girls dioptres cuts young
the earth's staphylomas pun.

Copyright by Feynman poly.

PLANT SYMBOLISM AND FLORAL METAPHOR.
Fiction

Dispersed in bowed florals metaphors bridges your dead corpse
folk cultures And traditions awakes push.
Passed by panicked asparagus racks ,I will fire bamboo
Strong holds ,pains and born willow from have been misletles
hush.
Lands and no acacia earths will acanthus favours in that
acrimony crush.
Yourselves your alliums breaks them of making aloe peace in the
almonds powerless in amaranth globes lands and no
one is baby breaths much.

Copyright by Feynman poly.

<u>Conduit Metaphor</u>

Fiction

Sons of close linguistics congregations one of broken handed
Meta languages wounds the one sprouts mental contents
heavens shortened.
Returns to unfaithful conceptual metaphor stars will surely

declare sapir-whorf hypothesis reproaches sons to
often Max blacks roads broadened.
Deeds of unclad dead metaphors milks hands of the happened
polysemy backs places of sealed purchased theory houses
that defiles information records saddened.
People who dessert arguments souls she expected my informed
as differences that stresses a books that exists as
cultures and heritages of culturals my perspectives no
paradigms that contains a media hardened.

Copyright by Feynman poly.

<u>Illness as a Metaphor</u>
Fiction

Of his righteous critical theory just in the rejoiced victims
blaming ways souls.
Claiming to living disease cloths, me and cancer forgets these
from crying tuberculosis abandoned hoes.
Last one horrors aids plugs every last psychological traits
flashes boys and grounds shamed their own priested creative
disease gives your days loes.
then the ambushed passions you also passed punishments
blows.

For our finished Christianity edorns her covenant
hyperactivity punishment as sensitivities Samarians clowns.
Out from living aids and its metaphors adorns psychotherapy
on blowns.
Was the living camille paglia forheads like flints kirkus reviews,
my rebellion tells as clowns.

Copyright by Feynman poly.

<u>EXTENDED METAPHOR</u>

Fiction

Heavily is fallen conceits again lands has shaken analogy willed traps*.
Sounds of pit William Shakespeare dilated like a heavenly Romeo and Juliet's known and the shelter love songs preserves laps*.
Mouths of looks the road not taken housed, eagerly pondered hands oh captains compressed barbs*.
Touched the smoked pataphysics kindly is my descends non figurative stronger carbs*.
Israel to crush the fire sign theatres together rules of resided interactions fictional watches crabs*.
In my peace metaphors we lived by but if board originals sons slabs*.

Copyright by Feynman poly.

<u>FEYNMAN POLY AND HIS CHRISTIAN FAMILY</u>

ODE

I acquaint all mine to help my face.
I remember to give the people as now.
But any one even myself had a form I uphold.
I kill no harm as laughs and hyper corrections had influence
never jaded.
WE Are parts to read and colours coordinates we elaborates
our hound.
Smiles of lectures smiles that nails me to the future pronouns.
Sending services of warmpths and a shift.
Why won't I laugh but alas this months filled with words.
My consolations will dance with no doubts I establish a skinny
foil of goodness had loaded to roil me my scratch.
My family my genes we are healthy as DWMC home.

Our households even sons and daughters much loyalty to follow.
If you are close come don't forget that we are good.

Copyright by Feynman poly.

DISEASE OF THE FEMALE REPRODUCTIVE LEARNING

Fiction

You giving Israel learning lights and birth sex peace and doing
dex is not strengthened sez works*.
Rising of setting gynaecology although your righteous
oestrogen the holy formed uterus locks*.
As your rising hermaphrodites whose right holds eggs is no lying
vulva ducks*.
Cuts treasures vulva my templed unions is there gametes about
the commanded dichotomy bucks*.
Rocks from doged eggings makes like willed flowers to
opposites those progesterone rocks*.
those bare face cervix the tired among morning trichogyne may
know words of malaria sucks*.
Have sets monoecious ears to ovum listened to puberty trusts
in andrology welcomed*.
Thoughts one dioecious in the rut opened my doula awakens me
syphilis spoken*.
In the mistress made for characteristics back to obstetrics all of
perinatology opened*.
Turn in gynaecology not in intersection though eats succubus will
recounts disease of the social opened*.
Judgements to sterilize long your hearths to grasps gynoecium
fined*.
Your lowly hermaphrodites' generation's after carpel will fears
mother's of lined*.
On the love you as conception's there is sterilized his days as
bisexuals peace wills paroicous signed*.

Copyright by Feynman poly.

THERE IS A GIRL I LOVE.

It was a day of bliss.
When she sat on my laps for a kiss.
Her tender undies I miss.
I was overwhelmed for this ,
How she clap her thighs with mine.
Her smiles all are a sign.
Watching movies and taking brine.

She took alcohol and smile amiss.
When I teach,
Her smile makes me know no peace.
She sat down and look straight in my eyes.
My hearths flap with so many whys.
She is fat,
And her ears as audible as the bat.
Smart as the cat.
I said I love her,
Reciting musical bars.
I can remember the day she was sick.
And how often jealousy and dick.
But she is weak.

Copyright by Feynman poly.

<u>Put it on a stone pavement rest</u>

Fiction prose

My will bad had feet water joints takes away hops ditch of love *.
A busy lie had vain dress who shed drafts at hearths of public
trackways cove*.
Oh entrances had grounds of ways pave a knowledge tie but true
terrazzo had calls of floors dove*.
My dishonest tests of sets had net areas my will lay but full
ballasts no cries drafted hove*.
Our soul shoes of you banked a man's drafts but ability bolster
disturbed*.
My ambush foil had ability pole a wrong doing tag but things
stamps a treasured rollers bulbed*.

Copyright by Feynman poly.

<u>THE PURPOSE OF EXPRESSION</u>
Fiction

Bluffing sufficient tales like behind resolutions as modes careless must*.

If balloting had corrected abuse but leadings abused her subdivided actions to drive apology no human argument faust*.

But utility art's as equally attacking not as more beads draught*.

Her development boy cuts as much briefs not of broach may as cards slought*.

But distorted casts checks the child but to checkings shall be development that had been compliants droughts*.

And forces composes those types individual and even have conversations faints*.

Are mythical demonstration's, child's of designates as we developed from genetic device ,can take for nevertheless effected paunts*.

Copyright by Feynman poly.

MONTESSORI ON SPONTANEOUS PROCESS
Fiction

We have the ovations with hissing Montessori methods whom
drunken takes*.
I teach no treasures educators like perpetual marine bakes*.
My willed divers had needs if sealed statistician's flakes*.
She blows me candid as careless of conventional Drake's*.
who went out conversationalized with astonishments
conventionalised you upon free association like labors that
laughs makes *.
Love mechanicals but divers monets had natures like nations
race scene*
Snap ye spots we're therefore stylized our address of been*.
YOU come to explode the lions folkslores like a girl that that
covered her ideo motor scheme*.
I informally had an interjection of matrix like mug that spokes
slang gleme*.
We smile like philosophy Biros that speaks no desolations of
nothing's hearths tumours sleme*.
If thereby bravado like among deliriums who heard mutuality
like will and perseverance flime*.
You revivals went about like falling abscissions if this absolute
upon none abstracts not against expressionisms no
false acronym clime*.
No care adlib the saints and act of God If among acts out
hearkened ,actions have laboured ad libitum slime*.
Oh servants allolalia but salvations anagrams had counselled
anastrophes brime*.

Copyright by Feynman poly.

CHALLENGE

Is thermogenesis productional heats and warm animals
blooded.
Such thermogenic as plants watered eastern skunks of
cabbages lilies vodoo hooded.
And lilies pined victories explosive arcenthobium americanums
boarded.
Classified muscles to dieta methods induced one coared.
Its shiverings into atp cause kinetic energy that brown almost
currently eutherians Warded.
Only swined .

Copyright by Feynman poly.

AN ADULT FEMALE HUMAN IN MEDICINE.
Mother medicine.

Women courses of treatments are often ladies,
Dame emergency use of females,
Girls precautions the risk of lass,
Gal cures and negatives miss,
Lassie increase in patience who dowagers,
Chicks treatments is required for matron, broad if pregnancy
one of filly,
Gentle women smears are Colleen,
Wahine isethionates rather Karem.
Babe instructions of tart,
Materfamilias sweating empress flushes empress.

Copyright by Feynman Poly

<u>YOU WERE ACTUALLY DRAWING YOUR ILLUSION</u>

Earths usings that singings got but my delusions and granded perspectives.
How does the colors learn to impress the materialized presence of reality to have my designs to come in
respectives.
I fetch you when you appear with the relations of my points no later the smoke of the retrospectives.
My hardness sees your evidence with your forms that I catch but my distress had you developed when you met me in
my separated watching for my firms to be meditative.
It means that when you turn to fall the Greeks you have to carry me like the traditions of ideas and jokes.
Waiting for Jerusalem's engravings.
Copyright by Feynman poly.

<u>...A SOCIAL DANCE. .</u>

Bundle of pomegranate outside.
Originated in shells growing possible.
Certain persons are considered instance.
Life to the legend that the bird grind.

Wizard and witches herbs.
Concerned with uncovering of the indigenous temple.
Among the Paris of India.
Will not feel the stings of scorpions that dance.
Towards the north the regions cries.
Who hangs us a sprig ceremony.
And the antidotes to their stings dedicated..
Was concerned with the edibility of leaves.
Among others in a conjured barsons.
Isaac prospect. .
Copyright by Feynman poly.

<u>....NOT MY INTESTINES. ..</u>

I always collapsed, the voyages of in lustrous.
The anti-temporal have turn me to a crucial point.
Rigidity has abandoned me.
My shell of vitality, is doomed ,
Not my intestines.
Time has come to me.
Billowing the gain of wants.
Not my intestines.
I am used to eating a condition .

Oh....
Not my intestines.
Who is d Lawrence, who is wole soyinka, who is this Elliot, I do
pay homage to.
There is a literary position I am conversant with, these have
make me use my forth senses, not my intestines.
Personality has asked me what is my forth sense .I said it is in the
reality of marvels..
Position has turned, literature hence approach, my view is to
attest, a revolution.
Not my intestines. I am not slow, I am not the house of image I
only described dead part.
You can remove me .if you do you die .if not you live.
live love

@Isaac Prospect

<u>...THE SHADOWS OF CELESTIAL LIGHT......</u>

Many as the finest of the sky.
Blood drawn by the salvage dog's survey.
Sacrificed humpback and dwarf fly.
Allowed to emerge during praise.
They pay homage to the monster will.

The chileatans of American light.
During a lunar eclipses to keep will.
The kamchatkans brought fire from light.
Men who knew how to make medicine skill.
Held sun wise circular processions until the eclipses was right.
Effects to be dissipated was thrice hour.
The ojibwas shoot lighted arrows to keep tear
This probably is closely related to the ancient power.
He was thus the ancestors fear.
Dancing in the wind and dance with thee.
Except that coyote sway.
Contemporary event see.
The juice of the stocks rubbed away.
Two stripe competing for complain.
Social economic strata to denote the art of living recess.
But socially sanctioned mating chain.
Eastern woodland are especially what I bless.
The cluracan os often still.
To the alchemists of the middle tear.
Following the medieval rill.
Springtime expulsion of death declare.
It is believed that the cobra resigned.

Associated with the chthonic blow.
Is adorned in northern mind.
That the cobra lives a thousand flow.
To the skin to the poison night.
The authority steals.
In the horned sooty light.
A kettle on a mountain reveal.

Copyright by Feynman poly.

..HISTORY TRANSPLANT. ..

Just a touch of history, just a waistband of ability, I am
flamboyant to see the wine of the presence, I see the
flame of history, like a moving guitar string, emotions of war in
the past history,
When I move the handle of history makes me more enthusiastic.
~~~

My neck is long my time is limited, but my words never die.
Dancing bullets of the memory of ability and necessity.
Eloquence screens aloud the country music is played from the
mountain,
When bad becomes a reversal, with only a bit position I stand,
The phone of humour, is coming in the morning, and is left in
the evening.

~~~~

I see the queen drink from the cup, i see the king drink from it, I
am secluded, and hidden.
I believe the incredible, the mountain is aged with age, I see the
night crawling so wide, I see military forces and coupe, children
dancing, and children been remembered for,
When capacity becomes incidental, I only know of the
government, when I read through the cursor of Puritanism and
Nazism,

~~~~

I can vividly remember I paid the tax with brutality, at the little
dawn at Tokyo.
I was beaten hard, I never relented, I ate a meal filled with poor
and rich memories.
It with gun and powder in during world war..
This is history, repeating itself.
@Isaac prospect
~~~~

Mr Emanuel. ...

>>>>
But she told me she was tired of you,
Oh I just confirmed it from that babe.
I told him life goes always and he should live it all.
There is still time don't cry my friend even though you fall.
I have told you several times this had made me wiser,
No matter how hard the wall.
All he have all he wanted is you.
Oh but you left him babe,
Life is a text of time but that is not all.
She told me all about you,
Who do I find in the other side of the ocean I guess it was that babe.
But she said to me she gave her heart all.
The pulse rate of your heart has begun to crawl

@Isaac prospect

THE SHIELD OF HELMET. ...

Colourful linens,
of the sea and their mariners.
manned your tower's.
traded beautiful garment,
stand on the land,
were your rowers,
raised their voices,
of the graves,
fall into their own nets,
are stronger than I am.
of loyal love,
brought you splendour,
of royal and noble descents,
endowed with wisdom, reveals the deep things,
of gold,
ready to fall down and worship,
was strengthened,
the holy mountains,
into wormwoods,
made with a plumb line,

@Isaac prospect.

<u>To the Primitive Mind...</u>

Triumph is a world of delusion.
A conceptual presence is an aspect of a soul.
What consist of nothing is an intrusion.
Subjectivity is therefore closest to natures whole.
Charity is a shrine to existing borders.
Death is reborn with irresistible alones.
Eternity is a spark of glowed clone.
When you hurry pictures to creation,
We wanton theory that was.
Darkness is a slave to sensations.
Baptism is a force enchanted because,
Immortality has eager to continue.
Ideas are power at hand.
When you are not ready vanity is you.
The law of causation is a feeling of breath that is planned.
I give courage no illusions.
But the soul is born with a grasping lies.

Beauty and existing words are imaginations.
There is a soul that is doomed to die.
The universe can be a past that exist.
The duncan faith is what the lofty thoughts says.
But the atlas of faith walk in our mist.
Brief and powerful is man's life today.
To lighten their sorrows by the eyes.
In which happiness or misery see.
Sunshine on our part cries.
High courage glowed eternity.
My own ideas has fashioned desire.

Evil has become eternal truth.
Concurred faith is the key of religious fire.
Purged by the purifying fire of the youth.

@Isaac Igbuku prospect. ...
Stay creative. ..

{LIFE IS A TEMPTATION TO ME}....

Space between times got me adduced,
I pursue it as death excused.
My manner at hand performed.

Voice of life humans led.
~~

The day all-time is historical,
It is true to pursue the hearth's will.
Some strange youth are conventional.
As I commit the sins of the physical.
I maintained a character so social.
~~

Guilty and levity can be sexual,
When judgement and appeal,
If I had hated all,
Testimonies can be political,
Nurture of the world psychological.
~~

When commendation is traditional,
I could speak nature's rationales,
Braided by an affectionate gospel.
To pursue life universal.
@Isaac prospect
Today....morning

< ACCESSORY >

...antonyms. Poetry. ...

Adversary has called the essentialism.
Betrayal from the world around him, enemy attain an immortality, that it paid for.
Opponent of something alive and subject to time.
Antagonist key figure, standing behind that orthodoxy.
Deserter of total oppositions.
Hater succumbed to the dead.
Renegade out of shoddy mass produced element.
Traitor in their respective headpieces.
Adherent trumpet in the laryngeal pouch.

@Isaac prospect sum.

<IF IT IS IMPOSSIBLE>

Thus I have seen those men,
May I observe the differences and wide dissent of them?
My opinions were established.
And therefore great uncertainty in this place.

Sacramento and Samaritan the Hebrew not only descending from them.
The insomnia, Latin from the Greek.
And everyone from another deep.
Much for just one, that all can be in the right, it is impossible, but any had lift.
Prose....

Copyright by Feynman poly.

<WHEN U CONSIDER>
A PROBLEM~

The strategy of support, and the rewriting of a product.
To generate associativity, and to consider appearance.
Experience is an option of account,
Product is the branch of relation.
Transform a natural community to an expression.
Use the attribute we need to branch a name.
Result is to display a selection and a utility.
Associative query is also a predicate algebra query selects a tuple.
The result is forming relations.

Copyright by Feynman poly.

A DECISION~

An expression is decided, examples is more often accepted.
 She is an equivalent of a common.
I use her advantage during processing.
I call the log from the tallest candle light. I must account for her assumption, I have step to a database, that
assume the system of circumstances and the system of shadow.
My transaction is physical, and various error had been attest to.
The log~~
I used her stable perspective for recovery, and a content went overhead.
She had some loss but when she executed, a replacement.

Copyright by Feynman poly.

A NEW SHADOW~

I entered the point of the light I see a current filled with a crash,
I then manipulate because it changes a page in my hearth.
I approached a storage bank, it sounds as if I have lost a system
memory.
I have buffer the table, using a technique, the physical chamber
had craved for me only.
The blocks have succeed me totally, I then applied the principle
of checkpoint, information make me crave.

Copyright by Feynman poly.

A RECORD TO BE GENETICAL~

I assume the principle of even, there is another presence of
techniques for recovery. It is time for me to apply,
all the useful update. I started craving to the update. And I keep
an increment of log.

@Isaac prospect sum

<u>AT MY LOW EBB</u>

SO LOW,
So shallow, I am going out.
I am receding.
I decay, I decline,
This is a low state or condition.
I am falling from a better to a worse state,
I see the state or time passing away.
Oh low tide, as I sunk to the farthest ebb of the tide.
I mean the lowest ebb of the tide....

@Isaac prospect sum

HOLY TYRANNY~

There is doom that arise from the eyes,
The painting and the antiquities of days.
We remembered what contains our remains.
Time is finding the praises of your days,
Death and the things that sour we weeds.
If it is argument we affords.
~

We subscribe love for your tribes,
What we provide the goddess breeds.
She drowns with showers,
The fingers of the dead we kiss.
Your roses and your perfumes reeks.
~

The black withness proceeds,
Large rain hide in addition thus.
Speaking of false subtleness,
Your profaned thoughts I rents.
The blind foes heaven clears.
Life and the cupid eyes,
I achieve a commendable goodness.
When mortal makes excess wishes.

@Isaac prospect sum

THE CLOUD IS AN EMOTION TO OUR HEART

Allow me,
Into penitentiaries and time.
The corridors of time,
Timeless sun and you beside me.
Blinking silence an Angel.
But the flickering eye.
~~
This painting frenzy of life,
Raised to an alien life,
We are the monument raised.
Faces made in the mirror,
Horror,
We are forever.
~~
The sailor,
A poplar of water,
By the wind drawn over.

Manate of granate salamander.
Edges blur,
Lightning and thunder.

@ *Isaac prospect sum.*

<u>WHEN VIRGINITY BECOMES PRIMITIVE</u>

~

Come from the maternal uncle,
Family of a more primitive type.
Interest began to grow irksome,
To immortality that was possible.

~~

Less than it used to be.
Less force that she use to have.
A kind of worship and a feature.
Against sterility and impotence.
When her intercourse build an empire.
When circumstances become impure.
Then action judge her nature.

~~

This is the kind of attitude,
When we develop sexual fatigue.
When jealousy becomes loathsome.
That we embrace the sense of our wife.

@Isaac prospect sum.
Today.......

A FOOL....
Verse...

Am not a child,
I gave u command,
This is the structure,
So very narrow.
Learn to use your tools,
Why u always switching,
My thought is device consisting,
I learnt to leave within it.
I told you what I was capable of,
Never shurn good colours,
Ornaments are in form,
I have tune the television device,

I have just call the principle,
Locusts carrying soldiers,
The building curved inward.
Elongated desires turreted,
I learn to break a wall

Copyright by Feynman poly.

A PEACE THANKS GIVING
Prose

Of peace the valley the hostility gates thereof.
The violence walls and conflicts to the kings, thy war servants
and thy people, took fear up the wine, the
violence outermost paths the peace making horonites, the
diplomacy valley, consumed regional peace.
with fire the peace treaties to Eirene pass.
has pledge got peace chosen to set my name,
was Latin very so afraid,
to shalom the gates of the fountains,
by salam place is respectful thy countenance?
unto good will the king, the quite sires of this man,
and tranquillity mourned certain days, to aloha pass,
the rest in peace eyes,
set Wolfgang Dietrich a time,
the croeseid coin kings the Croesus valley, to herm dike I the
rest that does the works, the Agamemnon gates,
thereof.
the phonetic written scripts, the work's unto coinage is me.
the Agricola cozen is shocked, and war justice a restorative.
justice policy the blue shields cultural heritages, in war peace
international laws the peace makers terms.
thou sovereign states are thou god hath police power thy
servants and to gendarmerie thee from Egypt .
for cyber-attacks there is none .
the energy ground to Mary land passes, thy peace day name be
magnified the full bright of hosts.

Copyright by Feynman poly.

A Plea?

Human claw of a crab,
human kind in the mouth,
man in a pot of water,
humanities approbations and deals, humans regarded as the shadow
,
beings on a moonlight night.
world to the drums,
human beings shed their skin,
human race did not starved,
people emptying her pipes,
civilization tricks the fish in a pond.
gods causes swollen glands,
evil of liber,
divine rhythm beats signifies,
earth jumps over the buffalos carcass,
men which are expressive of group attitudes,
groups for slurs,
and realization of an old joke or migratory,
destiny becomes an assistant professor,
prosperity helps fugitive across rivers,
humanity sees blind tricksters,
humanitarianism accounts only for the origin.
Tears on the eyes.

Copyright by Feynman poly.

<u>A SEAL OF REAL LIFE</u>

A seal of real life,
or a succession of speech sounds,
stable and resistance,
or sighing sounds,
the preachers,
into the abyss of human,
the psychical or spiritual,
the immortal part,
a particular musical style.
what is lacking,
possession soul and feelings,
hearing Within.
reasoning criticisms,
rumours, tidings,
charity sympathy,
along the verbal axis .
showing good judgement,
in the faith,
from the passageway radiant.
Expressions that effectively,
in the brain is associated.

Copyright by Feynman poly.

<u>ABIOGENESIS....</u>

Prose

More complex impossible without the use of pivoting
movements becomes involved later on.
Lock with all this maths seems more complex use matrix,
of gimbal demanded a lot from the processor,
reduces the amounts,
around a director.
angiogenesis in sprites approaches the closet you could get,
use commands,
the blur about all that resource they have found.
use to be from engines or lark of it in the way you use commands.
could handle the lazy versions for a while,
to create the edges,
we will discuss, the floated,

Copyright by Feynman poly.

<u>AFFECTION</u>

For faith itself is subdued armour.
Despite the trampling march of unconscious ardour.
The coward terror of the slave attachment.
Their bad their evil care.
Shedding over every daily case.
That makes the mystery closeness.
Which leaved nothing to be purged concern.
For man condemn today to loose emotion.....

@Isaac prospect

AM THE ONLY ONE?

Baby why are you sad
all this night mare we had,
am nearer to you am not far,
loving you is a sign.
the dollar sign,
is what you had.
the story of my life is traced back in time.

Now I will smile
all day for now.
You will fly,
I have come to realise life is a firm trick.
Don't let them take your lipstick or clean on you like a mop stick.
Love your neighbour as yourself.
Not what you sell.
Stop dwelling in evil.
Not everybody cares.
Is better to be righteous, stop living life in illusion.
But they don't know someday you going to shine like the flame.
I am going to make this fame
right here but today.
I don't believe in wishes, heal my wounds suture them with
stitches.
Your friends can be a vulture,
you got no time but you got your culture.
I am unstoppable,
I am impeccable,
bros brown I am incredible.
I fly like the wild dove above.

@.........main know/Mr Prospect

<u>An Intrigue...</u>

Intrigue in politics did not go away.
Intrigued university and a secret police.
Intrigues a ride with the devil.
Re-entry indebted to the death camp of Hitler.
Wintry allegory to the human race.
Thin streak posture of detachments.
Flint creak away with the demise of fascism.
Twin creek stream of time and whirls.
Den Krieg a raisin in plum-porridge.
Increase a certain dwelling.
Histories would be complete.
Victories as a recantation of earlier anger.
Within reach taken as representatives.
With trees from the formal pattern.
Will, treat humanity that were instinctive.
This stream to vex man and to convert him.
This street steeping on pull-man.
Being freed from the satiric.
Big trees detached critical artist.
Fig trees grim and solitary.

Spring creeks wishes to avoid.
Wind break is not absolute.
Thin stream a number of reason.
Prince street crowd remains unchanged.
Sophistries is too vague.
Thick trees in the rigidity and formality.
Thin green world of apes.
Skin cream a body of a fiction.

Skin crease in the degree of depersonalization.
Mint green stillness and immobility. .

@Isaac prospect sum

AND COMMON ERRORS

And indeed filled with crumbles.
Although sometimes effects succeed which may relieve the body
of the present that fades.
Yet if they Carry mischief or peril unto the soul that ancient men
humbles.
We are therein restrain by divinity not of masquerade.
Which circumscribed physic for free.
And circumstantially determines the use thereof which make
me walk.
Physic commendeth the use of venery that I see.
And happily like a strong block.
Incest chartered,
Adultery bare.

@Isaac prospect

<u>ANTHOLOGY IS A POEM OF</u>

Existence.....
~

If I read the books of the dead, if I feel the sadness of the dead,
If I dream the dreams of the dead,
I will always have a library in my cerebral cortex.
I see the poet that is writing, I feel the pictures of what he is
trying to denote, I ponder on the ideas he wrote, what a lyrical
marvel.
Light shine on my now and even to the reality
The songs of lyrics resonates deeply, I ask myself what is making
him to think, and I conclude,

~he must be thinking on cause and effect,
~he must be thinking of the senses and the extra sense,
~he must be thinking on mind communication pattern.
I am used to this pattern, I am used to this pattern like I said.
When I sleep I dream of anthology,
I dream of poets.
Like I said I see the mutability of lyricism.
Anthology are adventure of reality, I want to be swallowed by the
mystery of lyrics.
I shut the door, I open the door, my brain is hard, and my brain is
soft.
I have known her as a code of knowledge.
I see people attracted to me, just a page of a book is enough,
It is enough, for unrestrained, knowledge. .

Copyright by Feynman poly.

<u>Art</u>

All arts constantly aspires today the condition of music.
This striving beyond the limits that neoclassical theory, resigned
to the acts seems central to the nineteenth
century, aesthetic theory and practice.

The title of her study should indicate that I think her
characterization of modernism, is one sided and flawed.
She breaks between aesthetic of modernism, and what came
before her may not therefore be so absolute, as I would
argue.
~

What brings her together,
Her presence is not to take each other's place.
Music as her quintessential part, is a source of inspiration, from
which others tend to borrow.

@Isaac prospect sum

<u>**ARTISTIC -CHAOTIC**</u>

Double rhyme poetry.
Happy Sunday.

Artistic of Jehu chaotic.
ethic sets in ambush ethnic.
fanatic they sets each other frenetic.
genetic down the sleeves gigantic.
intrinsic sometimes it seems mystic.

Rhetoric talked about that sneak.
Bombastic takes up a ceramic.
Epic you can twist epidemic.
Enigmatic to be filled enthusiastic.
Historic running down the idyllic.
Metric my nasty neurotic.
Pragmatic seems to me prognostic,
pack the blowing pig.
Septic or excuse sporadic,
weak fingers continued their angelic.
Barbaric In the soul big..
esoteric filled with people's gastric,
hypnotic hits me last ironic.
Nick does not matters nostalgic.
Phobic there on the floor photographic.
Stick but it's exist sympathetic.
check illogically perhaps cheque literature.
Thank u all

Copyright by Feynman poly.

<u>BEERSHEBA</u>

Songs of descent in Israel,
and the oath of Negev,
centre of eighteenth month populous Israel city,
songs of Jerusalem at dunams,
an established biblical period,
distance at telbeersheva,
I feel the settlement of ottoman Turks,
caught at British,
led up to the Australian light.
riding the horses,
who envisaged the state of world war 1.
I speak Arab,
and the declarations of United nations partisans.
~
whistle of Palestine,
you say you have a plan for Palestine,
I am afraid of the battle of Beersheba,
how strong is Israel defence forces,
on the independence of Sephardic Jews,

The toast of Mizrahi Jews,
the community emigrated from Arab ,
I love bene Israel,
and the Cochin Jews,
immigrate of Ashkenazi, echoes of immigrant, in the soviet union,
relics of beta Israel,
I see immigrant in Ethiopia, I just want to learn their game of chess,

I won the chess grand masters,
I will sleep in the home of Ben-Gurion,
I will attend the University of Negev,
I just tested Israel's high tech,
how fascinating is their industries.
Many troops of Israel, from an abandoned farmland of
Babylon.

@Isaac prospect

<u>Blood on the Moon</u>

An acceptable colour, evil omen the moons part become stroke,
During the earth's presence, a lunar eclipses, when the moon is in
the fifth impulse,
Shadows of omen, and shinning dully by refracted light, the
foot couple.
Such phenomenon, as she is of great, import, of any celestial tie.
Enone is power, so extraordinary as her eclipse or comet,
adventures yoke .
Her believe is to accept thought, which have bearings on many
life of grace.
Mirrored harmlet, often in her literature, horatio speak in horns
that unite .
Of fire among, stars with train of fire and dews of blood , feature
certificate.
The warning fall, portent of fierce event, before Caesar kills,
cleverness courage.

Copyright by Feynman poly.

BOOKS

Has more formation energy,
observes outstanding stories,
reversed thoughts about availability,
apologises rationalized happiness,
imprints personal needs.
accepts emotional exposition.
needs empathy stamped as arbitrary .is wiser in guidance,
encourage valid objectivism .
usually should mediate settlements.
@Isaac prospect.

But we slew, slowly as I shouted continue.
A fire of life whirling and a wandering star surrounds me .
Hurried and aloud, on my rocky shore of starlight. ..

Copyright by Feynman poly.

<u>CHERUBS..</u>

Within the steel ribs,
And low fieldfare herbs.
And dropping bombs,
With drifting may and rubs.
~

Who is it climb,
As air under dairy slabs.
Her ballad and squibs.
They went like lamb.
Grasping at her stabs.
~

Memory fled to the hub,
To the Labour club, as she drags it through rub.
Massed green of other shrubs.
With curly stones and cherubs.
Hometown to work as a sub.
Existence of light before it.
The cypress stood before it.

Copyright by Feynman poly.

<u>CHILDREN OF TABOTH,</u>

Children of Harem,
skills of instrument of music,
month's in Jerusalem,
priest of the lords,
ass turn aside out of the way,
things of thy law,
wilderness of thy doings,
words runneth very swiftly,
hours of our name's,
noises unto god,
lie in wait of thy soul,
pots can feel the torn,
conference in comely,
beams of our houses,
doves eye,
hearts with one of thine eyes,
bed is green,
city found me,
myrrh is my well beloved,

charms of thy necks,
thread of scarlets,
conclusions of the whole matter.
Copyright by Feynman poly.

<u>COBRA....</u>

Cobra from a beast marriage, earthquake can both cause and cure .
Regarded ideas are intimately connected.
Accompanied believe of people scattered .
Nature lies in the weakness of the school.
Imminent folktales of story and culture.
Conscious opening of the casks.
Fashioned giant from within.
Natural music of flutes and cymbals,
Recorded unchallengeable declaration, of an unfavourable omen
Future increase in popularity,
Merely touching couplet,
Lines mocked humility.
Artistic alba amicorum appeared in any means to defence.
Tales ruined your book.

Forgotten saccharine,
Interference entertaining the loose of code.

Copyright by Feynman poly.

<u>COMMENTS</u>

Trice the saints and widows,
nigh into the city.
preaching vision which he had seen should mean.

Coming to my feet.

....

Is on nothing, to behold peace as aims and were vision together
evidently entertained corners we looked on.
called the side together which gave hands grace of apprehended
surname .
the spirit of the blind on relief into constantly affirmed enemy
we turned with divers without the innumerable company
diligently written in with joy of repentance they escaped.
as a wild trembling the cup of foundation, of the earth hands by
the hands of the great deep.

in thine ears carried away captives.
his greatest brother by night a light.
I forgive their iniquity.
all they have done.
eaten sour grape that have done woes.
behold always a voice.
into life being done to reckon.
these little same servant.
in the night of priests,
I have put life upon a pavement.
not like those who slept with their fathers,
if wherefore I spoke.

just with a small people, time whose indignation had
accomplished.
Love shall come into you peacefully,
I say among them the prey,
but you have to me in the estates.
with the mouth that speak proudly,

@Isaac prospect

CRABS ARE IN THE DISH

Down to a meal,
leaves of the trees,
indicated that her stories,
contains an incident,
gushed from having lost,
her relations despite the blurting,
the type,
sit down to a meal
several by-line of the wind,
the ditches to the searchers,
found of ocean tides,
woman bending in the bushes.
having lost the story of the hero.
Philippine westward rewarded as a flesh,
was honoured,
the dancers ringed into the cup,
up the reputations to some degree.
an ignoramus the sham doctor,
a balancing parallel,
a horse and her lurk,
to some degree with the tartars,
the sounds and most familiar, collected and discussed.
the castle at the ends,
cognate with ,
a laxative, parallel to central steps cry open.

Isaac prospect@
Lyrics

CRACKS AND SLAMS

The aggressive and popular speech,
in terms of witticisms and capacities,
subject to classics of wisecracks.
we applied criticism of approbations.
and personal terms that is coined.

DANCE OF THE VILLAGES...

Treatise, the kitchen is in it endurance state, the dollar appear
inside the house is there, earth is a house ,
that dance in wake and sleep .
Mankind, with an office of giddleness,
Bit the noise that floated, the mountain .

Dark

I am immortality, I give the night a stone,
I am the king that jump through terror,
I left coincidence in the wheel,
my heavens is in the spheres,
in the middle I run at length,
she is angry in the light,
my bed is filled with mask,
my natural virtue is blind,
I have meet divinity with the dark, birds,
as dark as the heart of the night,
I am mischief that brings false event, i am ready to fight,
I gave birth to that long beak animal that conceive darkness, who
comprehended me, had his resolution in ratios,
I will jump ,
and catch the illusion that I dream,
I dream of my kind of city,
my city had pumps, whose creation was invisibly cooked.
I will give a stronghold a habit,
in it second form, I cut the mask with my last drop,
I give the horizon a soul, I gave chaos its slander,
and I took the discovery of the day, I am equality
in creation that considers returns,
I insists in the most specious mazim,

@Isaac prospect
Lyrics

DEGREES
*Fiction**

My degrees she has as constraints bleeds*.
I eliminates as fins *.
my coordinates as Cartesians seems*.
her constraints is exploiting her hymens*.
our rests she integrates like motions whose equations sees her
Newton's squares*.
but how ever your elegant sources*.
I introduced her efficiently her coordinates had generalized me
by fulfilled Jeremiahs that had conditions to me
placed current urges*.

will systems and physicals around configurations burges*.
names fixed this cities uniquely of particular purges *.
the formulas to transformations of constraints voices includes
had murges*.

<u>Dinewan</u>

The leading personified emu, who plays a threatening ear,
Notes of mythology, as chief of birds in new South Africa water of
huge corner .
Particularly a tribe in that of the eualayi, the pile of another.
His lost of wings is attributed, to the trick played where there is no
pillar.
By gooblegubbon, the bastard who was on him harbour,
His speed in revenge, the emu got the bustard jealous of her.
All but two of his twelve youngsters,
So that they could be destroyed together.
They knew the wing, and I would grow as large as emus, now
emus is the drawer.
Less eggs but only two was to be laid later.

@Isaac prospect sum..
....Wednesday. .

<u>Dissolve like brime,</u>
<u>Still yet I chine.</u>

My heart and yours cline,
I had no dine.
Telephone call from Jain.
The yoke of light cline.
Read my verses line,
They are not yours but mine.
I just hump at nine.
Like the forceps that pine.
Your flows are like shrine.
Not about the 666 sign.
Or the mathematical sine.
Love broke like a spine.
Hot eruption that stein.
Your brain like that of a swine.

I could remember I was tie In.
Our bond intertwine.
I am frustrated give me some wine.
Are you sure you are the true vine.
You are sailing to the west airline.

2
Were love and hate align,
That which you a sign
Was irrespective of the bank line.
Do not cross that bar line.
You want to run on the baseline.
I am not part of your bloodline.

You are choke in that blush wine.
My heart is at the branch line.
Took up my pencil to get to the forth line.
So Much attackers from the frontline.
But the ball is approaching the goal line.
Why are u digging the goldmine?
Neither a grapevine.
U need some advice and guideline.
Why don't u read the headline?
Faith got us incline.

@Isaac prospect

<u>Do not underestimate design</u>

I am the vision that renewal mobilized.
I can quicken the figures of circularity.
I am the world that futures and simplicity, process.
When the novels were read, it supress the comparison of
silliness.
Then I preface a way, I am the painting, of position, that submit,
........the claims of confession,
.......the service, of futurity,
.........the life of the public.

When preference had anything to say it seek for my remark, and
I give it the principle of continuity.
Words had no position without me.
The principles of deafness, were created by a flux, but I am
always part of the flux because the only meaningful conference,
is the conference of reality.
When I heard of bias, when I heard of an object moving towards
the light I created a pathway for her.

The force of grammar is descended deeply into the heath of
many, I brought out it ambiguities and I created a mind that
could support it cost.
When the future moves when the subsequent draws, when
creativity walk upon history, I breathe life , chance, and
warmth to it muscles.....
Upon the old, upon poetry, becoming a medium essays is
swimming with theories and relationship.
To discovery and proposition, I becoming, the giver of signs.
I can define the idea of language by a merit, I can support essence

by the user interphase. I can point out, a handful of famousity, by
the pictorial relationship of etymology. ....this is me called ....
Design. ....

....

@Isaac prospect sum..

<u>DYSTOPIA</u>

Is anxious Hypermetropia,
a man Nokia,
an unbelieving Cahokia,
a slave Opium,
an u believing Utopian,
to his Cambodia,
constant devotion Sophia,
an unbelieving Ethiopian,
to depart Mongolia,
that is from Macedonia,
little importance Mongolia,
any one among phobia,
this regard Antonia,
in their own funny fallopian,
very little Babylonia,
to Christ homophobia,
the wise economia,
Apollo's watered dystonia,
even examine fovea,
god has prepared agoraphobia,
the sacred xenophobia,
who makes Colonia.
words thought Patagonia,

that is from Monrovia,
in turn poesia,
the deep hypertonia,
really wish photophobia, are strong agnosia,
it grow Gropius,
man examines bronchopneumonia,
to be sparely spermatogonia,
let myself be controlled rhizoctonia,
not of speech aphonia.
word play poetry

Copyright by Feynman poly.

ELECTRON BEAMS MEDIATE IN THE FERMENTATIONS

Cathode ray less labile electrons group discharge tubes.
of sugars electrode to the directions voltage the course .
cathode of partial dehydrations.
the course of cathode ray tube.
examples with sodium magnetic fields.
Helmholtz coil in portions.
One teltron tubes cathode from him that hath atoms.
cold cathode adjacent to that crooks tubes.
Volts tertiary alcohols ionize, electron fields converted to a given
thermionic emissions filaments hath not filaments,
electric currents converts a given alcohol to a given fluorescence,
vacuum tubes secondary ones amplify.
Triode to that carrying radio transmitters, or by used electric
fields shall be taken away magnetic fields.
Of water electromagnets generalizations that cathode

ray, alcohols suffers electron microscope, fluorescence on alkyl
vacuum pomp.
Rarefied air stands electrostatic generators,
glow discharge of the relative reactiveness of electrodes.
cathode which in turn anodes.
atmospheric pressure halides from an induction coin.
kilo volts of a methylation geissler tubes.
neon signs with amalgamated electrons glow discharge valuable
path to diffusions.
neon light having a terminal energy levels.
zinc sulphide can be eliminated from hydrogen, subatomic
groups without photoelectrons,
cold cathode, partial dehydration of hot cathode,
krypton's from adjacent gas discharge tubes ,alcohols with
transistors are significant oscilloscopes.
examples given dual manners,
converts a given beam well doing.

Copyright by Feynman poly.

fiction theoretical chemistry literature

AFTERNOON
THE HEAT OF VAPOURIZATIONS

Example illustrate the method of calculations,

steam has been cut off,

contents are weighed to find,

the torricellian vacuums, by empirical formulae,

drops of ether,

lowering of temperature, in the gallery,

of ice and salts,

ponds would freeze solids,

on the surface of water,

ordinary laws of reflections,

and determination of the refractive index

Copyright by Feynman poly.

EMOTIONS ARE TEMPORAL, YOU MAKE IT PERMANENT.....

I suggest it should be changed,
Her link must have power to manifest.
The desire which was suggested,
The desire which the great stressed.
~~
Nature had been received,
Thoughts that there is indeed.
The bodies of touch was not rejected.
Experiment of a man was called.
Nothing that was eaten was stopped.
~~
The vacuum that had been filled,
That air had been removed,
That the natural drive was applied.
It is a place I have stayed.

@Isaac prospect sum.

<u>ENDS....</u>

Prose

An intuitive star assumption leaves.

some groups the last sections of a troop.

communications by nights the prepositions arrives in the clear day at by logical kindle In them.

reasoning such as thee down premises of a land syllogism in heaven.

Your mind about brings sackcloth the acts of ending clefts something held of a rumour.

the temporal end to troop in the concluding times ends for this.

A piece of a woman something that is left in the heavens over after the rest have spoken being used upon all loins.

a small fragment of any language something broken of kindle in them,

from the whole captivity before their whole enemies,

a successful attempt at near upon scoring the fields.

Game of equipment up the needy consists of the drunks upon thy holy mountains.

Copyright by Feynman poly.

ETHICS OF MEANINGFUL RELATIONSHIP

Entries concerned with bringing poets,
This dream enables pound to make his juxtapositions.
Pioneer tree of identification and detachment.
Mistry portraits of man as negative.
Countries detached attitude towards the modern world.
Within three offered by the detached observer.
Wintry chronicle of unrelated event, increase within any one time. ....
@Isaac prospect. .

<u>Europe</u>

An etiquette,
in dollars or Europe,
being carried there by rain,
change it laws,
of the European union,
to think about it ,
just a patchwork of field,
on the head,

to find water and food,
dot on the map,
passage of lights,
that they deserved it ,
a passion with me,
features of faces from information,
the report is ambiguous,
especially in the magazine,
that you can repeat it at any time,
that you have done well.
true feelings,
go to pay for sex in prospect,
messaging the unemployment procedure,
one previously mentioned,
a circle,
is very easy to do or archive,
for anyone else feelings, in a series of flashbacks.
~

@Isaac prospect
Lyrics

<u>FEELING IS A PASSIONATE PLANET</u>

I read the book of the mind, influence is a spirit that bristles. The
larger circumstances unveils, she imagine an ion, my happiness
is in the life of the troubled and I will find the true man, I am
happy that the lightening, replied in my inference,
My quality suppose reason, feel a conceptual approach, my mind
see only the fire, my colours, maintained a gradual
attribute.
I contain a study, that avoids fallacy, I converse, why is it that we
love ourselves, I am asking by a feeling,
once the eternal lived at the real instance, it is seen to be a sphere
picture,
The principle of my nature, as the appearance were direct. Time
is not single in my place.
Worth is a certainty in me .
I only believe the fame of mysteries, know an extended topic,
which have a flight response .

Copyright by Feynman poly.

<u>FEELINGS</u>

I sending my greeting,
your love is intriguing,
me and you agreeing,
sometimes when I am seating,
I am use to policing,
why are you creeping,
why are you fleeing,
your love is ageing.
our heart is gleaming,
me and you no defeating,
love is a real thing,
baby why are you cheating,
your words Are briefing,
your talk is relieving.
don't be seizing,
when I call you it shows retrieving.
you have sow now you reaping,
your kisses are shielding.

Copyright by Feynman poly.

<u>FOLKLORE /MYTHOLOGY/LEGEND</u>

Tablet 11
Prose. ...
Immediate and future,
in early cultures,
severe winter colds.
In the barns,
he still supports the world,
mucus of his mother's nose, .
regions were it is found,
contents of the cups are shown,
in the clapping,
occasionally been discovered,
the brief rules of Maximillian,
absence of his husbands,
in the music's,
was driven underground,
for the species,
in four days,
so beautiful,
overtaken by her pains,
to divert the waters,
to every old accounts,
handclapping dance.

@Isaac prospect. ..

FROM THE LEVY BODY HEARTHS.

Fiction.

Are the praise before dementias in their honoured vengeance
dementia with Lewis bodies holied expanded Parkinson's
for his swords on disease dementias the man should*.
have been given promised neurons coming early married
Lewy neurites its listened could*.
its like crowned centrals nervous systems not so wise
autonomous rage is love would*.
the desirable loved synucleinopathies tries to penalty sleep
disorders pleasant tests bowls virtual hallucinations to councils
prevails becomes hungry*.
inclined your lips words mesh your eyed poisoned
pathophysiology meditates spoken at eared alpha-synuclein
hacks life despites your misfolded proteins sundry*.
I had toiled despaired Alzheimer's hates for a pained caregivers

to all although antipsychotics I will bereave fun dry*.
they have eyed anxiety housed and peace paranoia no one
disciplined posthumously to coming scoundry *.
saved me for jama neurology roasted made the attentioned span
hands will ,the golden girls had opened zephyrs *.
giving seeds featherstones like engravings and directors shares
your halved microbiologists emirs*.
concerning this a stranger chronic traumatic encephalopathy all
this great clefts shaphan and exiled sleepwalk with me they
must y marriage makes him armied dires*.
into captained hearths neuroimaging's kings of mourns all the
Babyloned clinicopathologicals crosstalks through doubled
dominions cases atypical in hearths sires*.

Genre: love poetry

I BECOME YOU

Please give me your strength, I will remove away my guilt.
the people can be my pain that you got stuck for
it is not over between us.

Look at our sons the good sky.
the sanctuary were you decide to reside.
I go weary and seeing thoughts of bulls and horns I have let you
in my books so I can see us together.
my fears your will as strength that cares.
my overconfidence is on earth when you come near.
I love your turn as my helper you are in my heartbeat so I do not
wear.
let me show you to my servant you are my comforter by noon
times.
the dream and its fullness as love cares.
you are great in the integrity of your kiss.
oh turn and hold my wills.

<u>GREY WOLF</u>

Troubles spoke as canid.
the boat of bread and fox.
in the kingdom of canis lupid.
troubles the courage of the grey wolf.

who replied something to the coyote.
many have seen the green jackal,
eat the loaves of a grey wolf.

He dammed the language and had been peering out through the
small window and he gave the door.

Copyright by Feynman poly.

HEART AND SOUL

EPISODE One (poem)

Heart and soul unites the fragment of Elliott poems, providing coherence in modern literature.
Heart and soul innovator in prose,
Heart and soul least speak of inventions of a new form.
Heart and soul lying everywhere so popular, heart and soul rubbing her teeth with wood,
Heart and soul postpone her husband death.
Heart and soul begot worse monsters.
Heart and soul discovers the guardian spirit.
Heath and soul set adrift in a boat .

Heart and soul regarded as charm against future evils.
Heart and soul fasting from meat and salt.
Heart and soul involving seclusion and isolation.
Heart and soul involves certain purification acts and instructions .
Heart and soul stumbling or falling,
Heart and soul drank up the ocean.
Heart and soul renders poison impotent.
Heart and soul exposed in a hiding place.
Heart and soul represented in the shape of a wrinkle faced old man with long fangs and cat whiskers.
Heart and soul cast upon the shore without eyes.
Heart and soul went around creating the universe.
Heart and soul becomes the ancestors of all elephants and caryatids,
Heart and soul with the fertility observance, on the hills on midsummer eve.
@ Isaac prospect sum

HERB...

The things she said is a strain,
Was it not her weakness?
She is too tough with freedom,
So strong to love.
She could, work,
And her body implies,
Strength, she gives me the faces, of matrix.
Her power, plucking the stripes
!
The fishes have been compressed, the light of strobilus,
Join the stem .
Hardiness, bent down to freedom.
The pencil is moving, she have to reconcile, the patent, in what
title is the form,
Still tough and going,
Physical force of fenced strength, the heart of a cattle,
Respect of her blood cell is concentric,
Sliced the reversal of movements so thin, nor the hater desire,
That wilful lily,
London strong and stubborn,

Like the herb of conscious respect.
In a handle that is favoured,
To a firm we impact.
Literary that her courage is mighty.
To force what was used.
Series and a bone, using a person's method.
Or tissue on matrix,
Strike more at stroke.

!
Penalty accepted a pass mark, delivered a kick four times,
World dominating the enervation, marine of her large tropical,
Of her love going west.
Or the host granules,
Harvest cutting or drosophila's.
Matter add organic series ,
subclass divided into another subfamily .
Two veins of region, the collateral to text, the rise of clinicals,
Vein the innominate base.
Pearls weight for secret tank, holding the atom.
Of a member, during degree intervals, first in the soft altitude.
!And resembling shagreen, being one indicated,
In love sticks a condition,

As function of a word,
Which reality has stirred.
Or unleavened flour.
Books of the condition,
Built source have thickened.

@Isaac prospect sum.

HOME

Preserved for us.
of warfare,
undefiled by sacrilegious invaders.
of the vastness,
of that dauntless city,
for petty ends,
of heavens will shape itself,
of tragedy does, in present shapes
of existence,
upon our refuge.
of a universe.
to those brave warriors.

I AM A DEVICE, I AM A VERB

I am a sentence that is not forgotten, I am the star with a verb.
The energy and the enemy comes to the place of punctuation.
I am the house that contains the definition that is very relative
By,
~ Accomplishment and
~innovation,
~linear continuity.
I am the invention that is preventing the comma of
non-revolutionary and unconventionality.
I am the innovation that comes to your
~
Present making,
When the insects walk on the street,
I ignore the unrealised oftenest.
When I return to semantics, I am the
qualification, the little link that is an equivalent of me is the relay
Narratives and superiority.

@Isaac prospect sum........

I AM THE ZONE

I am the zone you can't escape,
my days and time are heavy,
you can't run away from my custom,
I am the measure in ancient and now,
my hair is fresh everyday, I have capture her in the secrets, with
grasses and blue clothes,
I precede to her head, and the most sensitive part of her body,
I go upward to see the future hiddenness.
I reveal the weeds in her eyes, and I can see her cry,
I exposed her hands, to my greatest brightness,
my space she can't escape from,
I am peculiar I heard her shout and look,
I touched the vegetation,
I bit the soil, and I vaporize, the nutrients she stood upon,
my recurvation is great,
because,
I AM THE ZONE "

@Isaac prospect
Lyrics

I BECOME

Similar method applied to human behaviour.
We are used to physical behaviour.
Life sometimes can be a dead matter.
Wisdom make the duck go into the water.
~~~

Life was always put together,
But you have to be philanthropic to the poor.
When people crave for honour and power,
This is true however.
Time is coming is in the meaning of the letter.
~~

Voice were speaking of matter,
Time which obeys the indestructibility of matter.
We should live our life in like manner.
When the ordinary is an underground prisoner.

@ Isaac prospect sum.....
~~~

I JUST GAVE AN OPINION AND THEY FURY

Analogous as I knew, my relations concerning other plants,
And such is mortal.
Are they smooth?
Of which I came near infinity, unto this.
I have made it currant.
And as I have been.
I pass more easily, who is among us for the same effect is good.
Delivered of tiredness, by what Josephus said.
Concerning my root,
(poem)...

@Isaac prospect. ..

<u>I SHINE THROUGH THE STEPS</u>

I am the glory, in the sight of the light,
I read the dictionary of the power whose light were bright,
I conceal the angels I don't see ,
my nature, had it own rank and habitats,
I give the innermost room its imagination,
I am not afraid of death,

my sight is ready for nature,
I believe the reality of me, and the unrealistic pressure of the deam.
I affirmed the existence not to destroy,
I will climb through the stairs, because my eyes is in the heart,
SO I SHINE THROUGH THE STEPS
~

@Isaac prospect
Lyrics

<u>I</u><u>DENTITY YOUR COMPETITORS</u>

Who is the competitors,
today we have know the competitor,
competitors with main benefits,
what is that potential,
potential that had more to spend,
order had it benefits,
can you amount such money,
money obey the principles of benefits,
an acceptable certainty of advantage,
when we give some amount,

asked a question of importance,
competition equals extremity,
compete with good alternative,
growing when deciding,
took what we spent at levels,
their times grows like lines,
vocations with business not carnival,
ship a certain advantage,
being more or less a service or product.

@Isaac prospect

In America

We live a life of science and technology,
There I saw our Donald Trump,
But I am anonymous,
I just want to make fame.
~~

Fame like I said , is for the brave, don't think of it if you are not
ready.
But when you ask me that question,
What I said is that I am ready.

Ready for fame
Ready for fame ready for fame .
Ready for patriotism,
Ready for colonialism,
Ready for socialism.
Ready for imperialism,
Ready to talk the bull by the horn.
Ready to kiss the dust at any time.
I am ready,
I am ready.
In America, we claimed superiority,
We beat the base and the strings of creativity.
We channel the duct and the hearths of population.
In America,
In America,
In America.

@Isaac prospect sum.

<u>LOVE SERMON</u>

Movie poetry.

Like armies of accounts and evolved play,
Our ears of lions and peoples tests,
Here is a house like Edie,
Who went away to see Simpson,
But all the swords had jaded.
Like storing a good apostle,
I had to surround Oscar,
Like seeing her fronts as apocalypse.
She said if I understand the books of revelations,
And also stands the tests of revelations of Saint John the divine.
Then the vision had to be seen in America.
There is a male as an ape,
Who was territory used by Stanford binet tests.
Her times and visions at the plaza,
Like grease fund of comedy.
when it happens it becomes play right.
Whose ends had been so cantankerous.
what about the causing of infantilism,
As an appointed gnoea,

With movements of brutes
As intelligence as idiots,
That had uttered saintly.

Copyright by Feynman poly.
Pictures... Bollywood pictures

FANTASTIC VOYAGE

Movie poetry.

He understand the treasures were Like wombs,
and I believe in the bloodstreams as gold become the vas,
I had to catch my trips,
Were the stupid ones sees the balloons.
Their eyes become the cruise,
If I had knew later the departure,
It goes like the ego-trips,
Where presence had the innermost tastes.

Copyright by Feynman poly.
Photos.. Bollywood photo's.

KEEP SAYING YOU'RE WHERE

Composition.

Stars and suns of mould penicillin,
Glory and the land of the sworded penicillin Rubens,
Like mountains that filled penicillium.
Had she silenced the monsters of Alexander Fleming.
your covers of darkness and foreign meningitis ,
King's and strong nature of Ernst Cain.
with sounds that brings you along physiology of medicine.
Keep saying you're where Egypt and antibiotics resistance in casts
thou hall of spores,
Uncircumcised like fire.

Copyright by Feynman poly.

WHY WORKINGS

She lives in the hospitals at my lines,
even at Saint Marys closets to the mirrors,
She knows why workings seems not zeros,
Like sir Alexander the physician who is so bold,
If I see time to experimentally mould.

You with the first present of cold.
If he had named me to knowledge I tend to see variant between
lips,
A moment of me in attentions, like forefathers of clinical trials
had to read...like substance and withness seed.

Copyright by Feynman poly.
Draft ..

THE FANTASTIC FOUR WERE KINGS WITH SWORD

Composition

Firm poetry copyright Feynman poly.
Moving down of thoughts and sculptors at hand ,my frames were sparks of touches,
Her welders goes like statues,
My foots were epics of acts scanfoldings but generally around moguls like business,
She extended my hands but sits to intertwine my columns like DNA that had faces.
Her chiselled is angular,
So perfect,
Extremely perfect like past that had sparks.

My head went towards time ,
Your atrium had shut our headquarters ,
I designed.
But she inspired to speak awe,
She is high to open life ,
space but I exposed the structural pasts,
My elements is obviously an aimed,
Like time cried out visitors,
She creates my feelings that takes smallness to put inadequacy.
Wealth glances her sons' readings but looks were little as nervous,
It is good to have a thing,
You should be working by doing the right thing here.
Kings were seeing your statue,
Figures were deep ancient voices,
She had pieces low as darkness.

Curtain.
Copyright by Feynman poly.

<u>BLADES OF ARMS</u>

A movie demo of mine.

Scene......

Raccus in his writing table wondering how penicillin could be a blade for life.

.... raccus.....

Why should the care takers had we spend our arms but as our life's were like craves for crying from mothers chest at the daylights of labors when his silver linings had the blood offer you, so she gives us an awakening alternative of stage
with enough talk to watch me and its time
 with you an exclusive of we stepped so swift out of the chest ,
Of the invasions as shadows of death shall be.
....Tim........
Am I that wild or am I he who counts that I just sit upon the first and the last to say the seal cried out loud with whispers?
Sire.....that we should not deer have those trees I have been thinking of for long.
........(the illusion of self raccus)..
Sir this is the first demo what is your take on it do you like the Frequency

Copyright by Feynman poly.

VAMPIRE VS THE BRONX

Plot poetry.

A group of young friends from the
Bronx fight to save their neighbourhood from gentrification...and
vampires.
Composition.
As common as the feuds had bouts,
But the herringbones, had the man like the Lester's of coyotes
like pizza and race that roe me the western traces .
Had the Asians to live the figs in the generational chases,
Non knew their statues but like apes and hades.
Had the birds to gin the pages as Yankee in the rivers of Alaska,
Reactive argons and Anglicization that aviators of hers impacts
cages.
Go above the bags and bit the sages.
Copyright by Feynman poly.

PhotoBollywood photos

<u>MY HEARTH IS SLICED IN TWO</u>

Sad poem.

We were ten brothers but only me survived ,
We were ten lamp but only mine is seen.
We were ten brains but only one whose ideas are seen .
We were ten height but only mine was measured ,
We were ten laughter but only mine was judged.
We were ten players of bloodline but oh were art thou.
Solemnity......
If I could talk to the remaining nine,
If I could feel the pains of were dwelleth thou.
If I could kiss your reality ,
If I could kiss your colors ,
I am mad in my closet when I see only your illusions ,
THOU brothers ,
Thou brothers were art thou?,
Am lonely with your dead bonds far away ,
Cries and sires I miss ,
Let memory live me in the lutch.
My memory poem .

Copyright by Feynman poly.

<u>PLUNDER ROAD</u>
Firm poetry.

Railroad had to enclose me a load to relieve me of the boat that
had a repeated download as new host and welcome abode
whose family had to explode the virtual blow,
But keynotes as sensations important swallowed the animals
of the hallowed prompts whose tentacles shadowed and
rolled me up the scapegoat as a battle.
But free load and the larvae hard the armload to be rhetorical
but I re-echoed the marks of the strode to have a quotation ,
I over shadowed the areas and the promissory notes of morals
at the side of the road and squadrons of the anecdotes akin my
tag but the scapegoat had to tackle the embargoed city of hard
crescendoed at the tip.

Copyright by Feynman poly.

Sudden fear!

Movie poetry and prose.

Abrupt but the person with the blow had the sensitivity as once he knocked me as the overnight has the cells to be sharp as a kind. My retrospect as the European times has my supports and the touch had to be preserved as an acute quality with the opponents of apostrophe as a dozen.
My ashma welded me the avalanche of fortitude as a bang rolled down the burst that lived on the blaze with no hair.

As bombshells of the intermediate has braids or chiefly were the catches to the combats of Cinderella of a crement claps the phrases in acting of eureka but as ends and faced to him as jazz. The emergent had the pasts but epilepsy is sick as the ship of ejaculatory ticks had Eden tales .
As ducks of decisions and intellectual deflagrates so strong a splitting of darts whose saviours had the culture shocks of military to collapse who felt resembling emergent are claimants of editors.
End

Photoprompt Bollywood pictures.
Copyright by Feynman poly.

UNDERTOW

Movie poetry.

Undertow,
Sea paused at shipped sea puss by having rip tides an amounted
maelstroms the naval backwashes with a vortex in biological
seiche flotsam heavy ended whitecaps .
But quality shallows commanded my ended under tides of
manners with balls cross currents a dealings of qualities and
eddies I see.
But cameras needs tided relieves but wrong thermoclines
suggesting an upsetting muddiness intentions.
But relations subsets is timely as difficulty spume others with
Intestine gust forces.
But language shallows juices the secretary tides as disposings ,
In periodic points sensitive natures footballs schools uses full
tourches of cones.
Iron to everything of practical terms for Venetian cows driving in
drums of wooded ballistic finger printings to strong February for
tacks wins .

To the eponyms by reservoirs bulk wheats bents fastens carpets .
When quality designates or stable index of welded crowns beafs
in man .
Values from equilaterals until aesthetic surveys to senses of
Adam In natures.
AS EVERY BULLET IN CHICAGO HAS HIS NAME ON IT.
Movie poetry.

THE BIG HEARTH
Movie poetry.

As hairs backlog a wailing spider as one dames ,
The flocked bosses ,had courthyards caboose the places of vesta,
But people must astra,
the majestic cupel,
There came the dandy he left Franklin stove at the cry of the
salamander whose objects crucibles terms the forcus .
And mantles of hooks with aorta of cannonades of devastating
fogs,
Anger oh Asia,
Of inhabited artillery fires had escaped Asheville ,
My earth with arnica cord folia (Heath shaped)....whose flicks of
arctium lappa (hearth shaped)...the nations adorned.

Copyright by Feynman poly

<u>SLEEP MY LOVE</u>

Movie poetry.

As love liked gives him a song to sing ,
As ache has helps bangs his triumphed bed,
But else bunks among that music's call's to rescues jazz like sex
had love asleep a good apnoea,
Whose hatreds of ones awakenings had helps but salvations
berceuse to consider a willed carrycots and glorious conciouse
that resists cradles of love but tongues.
Deeds surrounds what wicked dreamt as opened.
But guilty heaviness had observed hibernations considers as
melodied hushaby hearths that attacked insomnia
response.
But a resisted lullaby as among narcolepsy are registered
obdormisions gives his red eyes as of guilts loyaler as steadfasts ,
rouse judged all guilty bags .
Awaked a dawn of thanatos praises silence torpids ,men stands
succumb,
Rejected armies were evils forms logs beings harps.

Copyright by Feynman poly

<u>COUNT THE HOURS</u>

Movie poetry.

Her gaze countings and pledge ticks but her sleeps thicked my tracks after it had been all.
Bells of life changes my means clocks as she inclines credits of the cinnamon eights to make us seven but her foots had the attentioned units crooked three as footed offices like every treasured abacus.
And ages on barons like body counts will catchers like beats for ten.
and points nothing rates of reckons or scores in some is tally.
A pique or numbing in nose counts comes losts of linage have expectancy and laps of the laps clean equinox and rewarded dingdongs of transgressional dials in with dawn bitterness knows chimes persons of herrncuter secures in paddles rescues zeros.

Copyright by Feynman poly

<u>CRY TERROR</u>

Firm poetry.

Her gifts of the screens among screeches the shrieks and
screeching but whooped who numb all wolfs of alarms .
And strikes the apes and cry out the freezes my stampede
reproach boo.
the exclaimed deep fore closed arrow its hoe and outcry my
jarrows with roar horns whines but alarium increases
acoustic phobias and brigades rose swallows altritions .
Redeems me on buzzers found none distress none answers me
from crouches ,you know my emotions lets the grovels subjects
may Homer foers disgrace liberation tigers of Tamil Eelam
mouths over sympathy.
I am for quivering's hearths those who red brigades you objects
of replaced Tamilr tigers as covers tornadoes which had recoils
whose hastens phishings on faced hue and cry to
morning crouches willed his huer and his presents.
Photoby Neville brand....

Copyright by Feynman poly

BE IN THE HYDROGEN

L had the equivalent of its form to be in the hydrogen bacteria of which I see it's chemistry but thus the mirrors had to be tetrahedral and images had the capitals of translations to be as a carbon of stereoisomers but as glucose whose enantiomers were in the terms of absolute values a group of configurations had the chains of the physicals and reference with optical activities had the equipotential of racemic that flips towards the steriocenters at a distance of the organic predominant but compounds whose cases of asymmetric sees the methyl as carbon had the repulsions of sugars to be at the nuclei whose differences of acids had to form the improper stability at the axis of solubility.
Fiction

Intellectual Adult Entertainment

Calculus that had the calamity of the dentistry to bleed and beg
the dental plaque to be receded,
But saliva had the prayers that the teeth had to confess,
as gingivitis around them kept the sulcus and its city.
But that lingual had to entreat the mandibular join my feet but
the anterior was successful as bad breath had my face to the
receding gums of that evenings but chronically we know the
power of the periodontal was so sick of a scaler king that even
potassium could cure but bi tartrates had to mention a cream
that Is upon the tartar of those sack cloths whose calcium had the
saving cold but phosphate must work so hard for proteins to be
mortal and lipids to be the immortals of the salivary nature's.
That says that the microscopy are deeds that pays more oxygen
but I had to cut the periodontium in Jerusalem of buts.

Copyright by Feynman poly
The immortals ...

SCIENCE PROSE DRAFT
....learn to strike....

Cardiac must learn to strike by catheterizations at the movable bikes but greater Sabbaths like the occlusion of love blessed the ischaemia of a man of the angina whose guides breeds me like the stenosis of curves ,

My coronary hard the guides of retrosternal to land me in the plaque of those eyes of rupture at the beeks.

But shoulders had to see me in the arms of the volts like the exertions had perfectly increased beyond the takes of demand but so lawful at the central place of love by crushing like the straws at the chest of the balls .

But how profuse it seems to the call.

Creative writes.

Copyright by Feynman poly

<u>CHILDREN SHOULDN'T PLAY WITH DEAD THINGS</u>

Movie poetry.

Plot ! The dam was filled with dustbins of souls and Kira was
ignorant of the effect of playing with dead bodies .
Composition.
My eyes are usually box ,
I had to interact with the houses,
As playful as fairy,
A noise hell.
If evils hellhounds to somewhere to walk.
I decorated the pictures whose parents had family ,

As flooded streams counting,
The skies had rompers,
that flew with arrows of Halloween.
Rivers were like kindergartens,
Fire flared the detritivores.
they that had the desert counts.
Up the wideness of suggestibility,
In the cloud of rumpus room.
and rocked possums,
The trust of Orpheus.
That actually diddles,
In a quaked part of our triplet,
Is of a God and of trick or treat.

Copyright by Feynman poly
Photos ..Bollywood

<u>Monsters and Love</u>

Plot !
Abiku was in love with the three winged monster,
She had the hairs of a snake but her name is Medusa ,when Abiku
comes around he could not turn to a stone because Medusa the
creature loves him ,but when any male folk comes around
Medusa they turn to a stone.
When Medusa does not love them.
Movie poetry.
Composition..
For ever I had planted centaur ,
the earth of peace and fury.
To love as in boo,
In the night of acardia.
Assembly like oil and anglophilia,
OF official dainty.
As does the weather of grace,
His sleeps for hangers .
In between the rhythmic hearths .
As reconstructions had Hayes.
Of a trees happiness ,
Of official greatness of graecophilic ,
Trunks of distinct trees.
In a hollow thunk ,
In sacrifice, takes ones romantics.
To no wicked praises,
To all human,
does states as honors.
But records interprets history of whist hearts.
To criminals of spies of nests,

In an inverse reciprocal.
When my components quenches.

Copyright by Feynman poly
Pictures ...Bollywood

<u>SOMETHING WITH HOLINESS</u>
Composition

In religious nodes ,
Something with holiness explodes ,
Spiritual redemption coats.
Or divine will roads,
From the old English boats.
Originated in the Germanic paganism remotes.
If I exist in the islandic loads,
As process of christanilization road.
In the Biblical vote,
The Priestly blessings promote,
What may aldonai tote.

The rabbinical Judaism decodes ,
A blessing which acknowledged god flowed.
Blessings afterwards of the Jewish laws goads,
Like curses downloads, by giving divine services connotes.
Copyright by Feynman poly

<u>Dracula In love</u>

Movie poetry.
Composition.

Writing had start and stop,
With no idea to love.
Our work had stop but drinking never stops,
Our marks had questions,
All the puzzles had holy,
Jigsaws,
That had accompanied madly in framed love.
Of thousand Bollywood to prisoners breakfast if strong
neophytes,
May salvations stumbling.
If illusions and truths,
Had questions for tunes,
your touch Oh! dear,
Had quarks to consider who shows me life Bollywood's had
illusions and truth.

tag ..Dracula is in love with the rain

Copyright by Feynman poly
Pictures ..Bollywood pics

I RESEMBLE THE EQUALLY NOTABLE PASSACAGLIA

Composition.
Poetry

I protect the epics of kings ,
As persons of angler fishes and amusing rings.
As battled brachiopodes of hell sings ,
Of young composites afterpoles dings.
Like harrowing glands had flew bings,
Like crocodiles palesness in that day crings.
As disturbed aphorisms had killed me ,
Lol dance spheres had occasionally see.
With gods peafowl went down lee.
as similar urine had confound he.
Like china alabaster had discussed flee.
Like monstered evils had bitten cree.

Copyright by Feynman poly
18/5/2021

<u>EDUCATION AND THE DOGS</u>

Movie poetry
Composition

The roving foots answered ,
A womb of train and the knees.
I had weeped causes and the garments,
Like the vets you said.
As digged choir schools is hidden,
But vain eggs symphatized the heads of 'schola cantorum 'at twilight.
Composition time today Saturday.
Copyright by Feynman poly

<u>CHILDHOOD CANCER</u>

Movie poetry.
Composition.

South chicken pox itself but over child name.
But the kings groups is today.
What happens in cystic fibrosis of my will,
Half of impetigo to be divorcing.

From nations infants must have needs.
As those things which measles had lived towards.
But towards mumps oh rare progeria so marked.
she had composed retinoblastoma for life.
thou earliest infancy and stages ,
Had resemblance of haemangioma that released .
Her given verdue of lutches.
Went ahead but advanced and complex.

Copyright by Feynman poly

<u>There Came a Letter From Heaven</u>

Composition

I pay my symploce for him,
as you scatter the skies booms always.
If there is but and if there is yes,
then I had kiss paradise in peace.
Tell the news to the world,
that equinox will be hell soon.
All the Babels must be restored ,
the facts had yet echo good news.

That even strength and stigma had pride.
IF I hit the nail on the apostle's head with sin,
In cycles of lies and cycles of truths.
I had wrote the letters to devastators,
Along side the jooks of music's.
I saw the hooks to be worthless,
They kept in fastening voids,
Hmmmm alas!
Another kind of subspecies will be discovered soon,
As there came a letter from heaven.

Copyright by Feynman poly
15/5/2021

<u>BUT WHOLE VASCULAR INHABITED A SOVEREIGN SURGERY THAT SPEAKS</u>

Medicine movie poetry.
Composition

As landed arteries had dispersed,
The humiliating veins borne.
As therefore medicine not devour,
Your nationed clinics which will be cleansed .
But childless radiologists oh lords,

As world Leonardo da Vinci not clean.
But procedured sclerotherapy had ways.
As party endovenouse had gave plundered prophesy of
treatments that we produced.
YOU grained angiography to cracks had roads stentings of
prologues,
Of mistressed femorals into waterlabs.
As strength varicose of socceries ,
Like prided carotids with perforated seeds of rattled vena
cavae to devastators came.

Copyright by Feynman poly
Vascular surgery poetry and prose.

<u>BUT PRIDED MEDIASTINITIS KNEW THEM.</u>

Medicine firm poetry.
Composition

Ends to stumbled mediastinum musters all that comes .
But swords acute of fiercest.
As arms chronic as your daughters as festivaled emphysema like
towers fortified.
An enemy of effusion had the walls,

No rejected scapulae had kept,
You down as turned granulomatous exulted.
But compassioned anaerobes had done,
And morning X rays you killed,
You kept sepsis to survive.

Copyright by Feynman poly
Mediatinitis poetry and prose.

<u>AS WALLED SEPSIS OH ZION</u>

Medicine firm poetry.
Composition.

You resolved infections you stretched,
Your chemical immune systems had strengths,
As thorns of fingers among one housed body temperature to listen
like ashed fluids replacements to whom was weary she looks
like diabetics of emotions .
But saying that response syndromes had to be ashamed.
I had watched mechanical ventilations with no pity ,
That my cardiac output had escaped ,
with remorsed insulin that had thigh .

But pleasurable confusions had looks !.
To Kids through the skins for least from captured polymerase as rashes of named blood gases be of horses.

Copyright by Feynman poly
Sepsis poetry and prose.

<u>AS HERALD CARDIOTHORACIC REMAINED SWORDED</u>

Medicine Poetry.
Composition.

But carpet fields had to walk the time,
As seen medicine of Israel cline.
The place of surgical treatments is fine,
As rosed hearth disease whose mothers swine.
But surging long disease which you fine,
She sits on the pleura by playing dice.
Whose beared mediastinal had harboured the line.
As jordaned specialty with saddled brine.
You had opened osteopathic of silvered crane.
As deserted thymus those donkeys Dane.
Did water subspecialized in commanded bane.
Ye idle vascular had refined vain.

To mighty transplantations had pin rain.
those ships of bypass heavens hein.

Copyright by Feynman poly
Cardiothoracic poetry ...genre.
Fiction

SUPER COLLIDER THE BLACK HOLE APOCALYPSE

Firm poetry
Composition

She took her largest to be crucified,
Your sepulchre particles had the cryptic sears.
As kings colliders had the light,
The stoppings built of cloths.
But preparations of catastrophic had a soldier with garment.
She never malfunctioned me.
As I open to crucify him,
On writings his skulls nigh.
In gardened species thou rings threatened,
The disciple humans had delivered thugs.

EXCERPTS

THE LEVITATED CATARACTS REPLIED THE GREATEST SURGERY FROM OUR EAST

Medicine movie
Composition.

But upright lens fears a condemned eyed of man,
Who stopped cataracts of the gods,
Had companions of intraocular lens to cure,
I feared, vision shouldn't be bad,
And of each congenial I had laid,
To denied emulsifications like acts.
Of works that had the ophthalmologists,
To be patient.

How do you see ambulatory people reckoned,
Of a gazed per bulbar in her midst,
Come with ruin retro bulbar had vile.
Entire glossary that sees phacoemulsification thus far away.
But no inclined standards of care that left,
Your hindered extracapsular to run.
TO me disciplined haemorrhage of wine inclined.
But someone's sclera had signs.
your blazing cornea like fire ,

Of vineyard had femtoseconds of cylindrical sickness.
But swift Sulcus had to return.
But thousand cry extractions had lips.
Ah ,rods of subluxated had your angers.
But upon silicon you became strong.
Like Hundred commodatives becomes cares.
Like oaths of presbyopia had mankind.

I archived the Bausch and Lombs of the keen.
To the invasions of ultraviolent as Zion considered.

Copyright by Feynman poly.
Cataract Surgery Poetry and Prose

OF DECREED USES FOR SOVEREIGN TRIGONOMETRY AS RESIDED PLACES

Fiction composition.

In stringed trigonometry of envious depths ,
True for theory with looks with music of young's proceeds.
Praise rises numbers who crowded walks rises beads.
Are flying fronts of Fourier series the widowed songs.
Peaks with transforms tends commanded ,
Large houses of statistics of acts holy.
She drives caned arm 2 of going foots.
the escaped international with this spaces.
OF thousand stations who guided lords ,
In provided ages of exulted reasons of his peaks.
But cursed enlightenments the replaced watched.
Against rebuked Thomas Paine of utterly watched.
written of trigonometry being heated survey is giving armies.
With angered mountain Everest of increased yokes,
had nights of logarithms squares weeping killed.
Drenched and prosthaphaeresis treachery traps.
Hearths among music glorious places.
rebellious among acoustics the scattered architectures giving
raged astronomy with shames appalled .
THE daughtered cartography came winged creeds,
Of reproached optics inwards thus drums,
Was foliage visual perceptions from punishment rebelled.
Her younger Pythagoras he broke pages.
Of testable sine as your practices of youths waves the despised.
Came top climatology the justs,
Your prides heats were lives beeps.
Planted abundant diffusions those with feelings ,

Off its digital compressions eagerly vined.

Mouths when unequally lows only sodom.
Of some Eigen values branches vines.
Long plumage oscillations her gathered musts.
And his solutions justified your dids.
In mixed morbius or else crushes parts,
so would complex the served toes.

Copyright by Feynman poly
Welcome
Genre .....uses of trigonometry poetry
Written this evening ......

<u>At Least Partial Fractions Decomposition of Generations Certained</u>

Abstract
Composition.

Came peace algebra but taken parables ,
The whaled rational fractions that ye denied.
think of heavenly polynomials to her sparrows.
You had known algorithms which is not fear.
Dances like calling rationals deaths had you against deeps.
Servants of discipled antiderivatives shall be your lords,
Because her Taylor's as wampth series valued her hairs.
Shall I hear inverse not before z transforms sittings had likened.
Confess, yes I confess Laplace calling you whereunto,
Days and kingdom denominators rather her body.
Hear her eyes and power despised of hearths.
there are your thou wind of numerators alas what had been healed.
Not as Poor Square free in all taken.
Were my root coefficients but really had words.
Fields as didn't indeterminate not as thou receiveth behold you without identity chokes to heal.

Copyright by Feynman poly
Welcome
Partial fractions in mathematical humanities poetry and prose .
Written......afternoon...

BUT SPOKEN THAT BRINGS SURGERY TO MAKE YOU FROM AMONG HISTORY IS WILL

Fiction composition

All thoughts unto kings away as the main medicine phases as medallions.
Secondary as world abstractions by what take him.
Then a prophets revolution midews as holy obstacles .
People and from bleeding pains ask me a law .
Declared her glorified infections asked as unclean.
Mountains that allowed Indians subcontinents gathered them over .
With her objected sushrata sucks out my needles
.Bearings as her acacia found me feeding.
Left no woman as trepanations holiness and messages
,Silent but over my dura mater passing my fears.
First is her world of cave paintings dwelling an account.
Pride as taunted epileptic seizures salts her wastes .
will I leave your mental disorders to plunder my remnants .
He will ,as indeed medulla had windows to thresholds.
Her account of one intubations had taunted to boast.
She destroyed a willed anaesthesia of heavens I crushed
To vengeance and loved inflammations whose unisons had utensils.
She convulses like manic psychosis that staggered as drunkards.
But timely as ultimately strokes had completely a plundered cream.
She mentioned me alone as codes of Hammurabi that sang a city.

As wines in mountained shekels had wraths to confront.
But pastured circumcisions had benefits spoils,
But on retinoplasty pondered a tongue.

Covered like braired plastic surgery cities as permanent.
Heads as dubious oaths flee my lane.
Spreads that rejected lithotomy sets away undies.
But against a judged ligature that said a hill is unique.
But swords had depths of yokes as eggs and life and time.
My errors had rose oils that recommends me.
But horns with blood vessels has warnings like heats.
No warning but upon tuberculosis life had persons ,
As mildness plaster of paris had you a worn.
To suffering of restricted amputations chemicals etched
himself.
By chloroformed allows contagious sounds of heads.
My antiseptics like sons asepsis had corrupt,
But please sterilize who left,
With taken medical gloves that rest had left.
She deserved raged black death of sovereign.
As crowns and stoned chloroform with every places
Of top fistula can punishment see.
Covenant of a stranger is alive as Shepard's ,
No hated brain surgery had punishments.
AS flocks and pericardia sacs with houses of holies,
My sea and parts membrane went through a bone.
But against an island, open hearts had drink your clubs.
But orders had buryings as a transplanted becomes a flesh to
eat.

Copyright by Feynman poly
Genre: History of medicine poetry and prose in humanities
Prose Poetry